Community Justice

Community Justice discusses concepts of community within the context of justice policy and programs, and addresses the important relationship between the criminal justice system and the community in the USA.

Taking a bold stance in the criminal justice debate, this book argues that crime management is more effective through the use of informal (as opposed to formal) social control. It demonstrates how an increasing number of criminal justice elements are beginning to understand that the development of partnerships within the community that enhance informal social control will lead to a stabilization and possibly a decline in crime, especially violent crime, and make communities more liveable. Borrowing from an eclectic toolbox of ideas and strategies – community organizing, environmental crime prevention, private–public partnerships, justice initiatives – *Community Justice* puts forward a new approach to establishing safe communities, and highlights the failure of the current American justice system in its lack of vision and misuse of resources.

Providing detailed information about how community justice works in each area of the criminal justice system, and including relevant case studies examining this philosophy in action, this book is essential reading for undergraduate and postgraduate students of subjects such as criminology, law and sociology.

Todd R. Clear is Dean of the School of Criminal Justice at Rutgers University, Newark NJ, USA. He is a past president of the American Society of Criminology and the Academy of Criminal Justice Sciences.

John R. Hamilton, Jr. is Associate Professor of Criminal Justice Administration at Park University. He retired at the rank of Major from the Kansas City, Missouri Police Department after 26½ years of service. He has extensive experience in community policing and problem solving, and is also a member of the Board of Directors for Synergy Services, Inc.

Eric Cadora is founder and director of the Justice Mapping Center. Prior to establishing the Center, he has served as Program Officer for The After Prison Initiative at the Open Society Institute; as director for Research and Policy, Court Communications, and Day Centre divisions of the Centre for Alternative Sentencing and Employment Services (CASES); and has also conducted graduate work at New York University.

Community Justice

Second edition

**Todd R. Clear, John R. Hamilton, Jr.
and Eric Cadora**

 Routledge
Taylor & Francis Group

LONDON AND NEW YORK

First edition published 2003

Second edition published 2011
by Routledge
2 Park Square, Milton Park, Abingdon, Oxon OX14 4RN

Simultaneously published in the USA and Canada
by Routledge
270 Madison Avenue, New York, NY 10016

Routledge is an imprint of the Taylor & Francis Group, an informa business

© 2011 Todd R. Clear, John R. Hamilton, Jr. and Eric Cadora

The right of Todd R. Clear, John R. Hamilton, Jr. and Eric Cadora to be identified as authors of this work has been asserted by them in accordance with sections 77 and 78 of the Copyright, Designs and Patents Act 1988.

Typeset in Times New Roman by RefineCatch Limited, Bungay, Suffolk
Printed and bound in Great Britain by TJ International, Padstow, Cornwall

British Library Cataloguing in Publication Data
A catalogue record for this book is available
from the British Library

Library of Congress Cataloging in Publication Data
A catalog record for this book has been requested

ISBN: 978-0-415-78026-1 (hbk)
ISBN: 978-0-415-78027-8 (pbk)
ISBN: 978-0-203-85580-5 (ebk)

To the memory of Dennis Maloney, the heart of community justice.
Todd R. Clear, Ph.D. and Eric Cadora

To Bini, Jenifer, and Jessica your support is appreciated. Also to my
colleagues Greg, Carol, Ken, and Mike for your encouragement and
professionalism.
John R. Hamilton, Jr., Ph.D.

Contents

4   Corrections and community justice   94

5   The future of community justice   129

Preface

This work is an updated version of the *Community Justice* book that was originally authored in 2003 by Todd Clear and Eric Cadora. It provides updated examples of community justice in practice and continues the belief that community justice is an effective way to build healthy, viable communities.

Community justice borrows from an eclectic toolbox of ideas and strategies: community organizing, environmental crime prevention, public–private partnerships, justice initiatives, and so forth. Each of these strategies has its own rich heritage and literature and it is not our intention to provide a comprehensive literature review for any of them. We hope that readers will explore these topics more in-depth on their own and we have provided bibliographies at the end of each chapter that provide suggested readings to learn more about these strategies.

Recent news reports in the United States have told the stories of budgetary cutbacks in federal, state, and local government. With these cutbacks comes the realization that criminal justice agencies will suffer from lack of funding to assist them in achieving their mission. Often times, agencies believe that they must increase staffing to meet the demands the public places upon their organizations. Community justice offer new strategies that can assist criminal justice agencies in not only achieving their mission, but also strengthening partnerships with the community that empowers them. While additional personnel are always welcome in criminal justice agencies, community justice strategies may enable these agencies to achieve more with fewer employees and better weather the effects of the economic downturn. With increased implementation of community justice practices comes more information that can assist criminal justice agencies, academics, and other stakeholders in fine-tuning and improving the delivery of services. The message of community justice is also clear about the need for the private sector and nonprofits to join the partnership to make community justice a reality. The authors believe that community justice is an exciting concept that can make criminal justice agencies more effective and efficient, but we also believe that it is the right thing to do in helping to strengthen communities hard hit by crime, poverty, and malaise. Community justice can be successful if the criminal justice system, government at all levels, the private sector, and nonprofit organizations develop partnerships to address the variety of problems that face hard-hit communities.

In this book the reader will find examples of community justice in practice and case studies that provide more information about specific community justice efforts. In Chapter 1 the reader is introduced to the concept of community justice as well as some of the difficulties encountered by high-impact areas. Chapter 2 examines policing and community justice and how the concept is already partially in place in many police agencies. Chapter 3 provides a discussion about the role of the court system in community justice. Because of the technical nature of the court operation and the traditions that the court system is built upon, many would argue that the court system cannot be much of a player in the community justice movement. This chapter illustrates how courts have embraced this philosophy without losing their emphasis on justice being served. Chapter 4 looks at the role of the correctional system in community justice and discuses the role of community corrections in community justice. Programs in the institutional setting are also discussed, helping the reader to better understand how the entire correctional system can participate in providing community justice. Finally, Chapter 5 discusses the future of community justice and addresses some of the more common questions that are raised about the concept of community justice. At the end of each chapter the reader will be provided with a list of suggested readings as well as websites that more completely explain some of the concepts discussed in the chapter.

This book would not have been possible without the hard work, dedication, insight and enthusiasm of Todd Clear, Eric Cadora, Charles Swartz, Sarah Bryer, and Joel Copperman, who authored the first version of *Community Justice* and brought forth a challenging concept for the field of community justice.

1 Criminal justice and the community

Community justice is an emerging, innovative idea about the way criminal justice operations ought to be carried out in places where public safety is a significant problem and criminal justice is a significant fact of life. We call these locations high-impact areas because they are places where both crime and criminal justice responses to crime exist in concentrated levels. Community justice offers a way of rethinking how traditional criminal justice approaches to public safety can be reformulated to help make those high-impact locations better places to live and work.

Two assumptions are inherent within the idea of community justice. First, it is assumed that within existing jurisdictions, such as states or large cities, there are critically important differences from one community to another, and these differences suggest that criminal justice strategies need to be tailored to fit those differences. The same criminal law applies to everyone living in, say, California, but criminal justice strategies, if they are to be successful, will need to take different forms in locations as divergent as the crowded and impoverished Watts section of central Los Angeles and the pristine, wealthy neighborhoods of La Jolla. The second assumption is that formal systems of social control, such as the criminal justice system, are not the main mechanisms of public safety. Rather, informal social controls – families, neighbors, social organizations, and friendship relations – form the most important foundation for public safety. Community justice, therefore, builds varying strategies of formal social control, depending on the particular problems facing the local area, and always has as one of its main aims strengthening the capacity of informal social control within that location.

High-impact areas are the logical targets of community justice initiatives because the formal and traditional methods of criminal justice have proven so inadequate in these locations. The criminal justice system identifies offenders, apprehends them, and imposes criminal sanction on them; but in high-impact areas, this focus on processing individual criminal cases through the justice system does not take into account the cumulative impact of these individual decisions when they disproportionately concentrate in specific places. In some high-impact areas, for example, more than 10 percent of the adult males are arrested, convicted, and incarcerated in any given year (Cadora and Swartz 2000)

However, the impact of removing these active offenders is blunted by the fact that an equivalent number of males re-enter this same neighborhood each year from prisons or jails. The collective impact of all these arrests, convictions, incarcerations, and returns can be a major destabilizing force in the neighborhood, exacerbating the effects of poverty, broken families, unsupervised youth, and unemployment. Without tackling these important aspects of community life in high-impact areas, traditional criminal justice is little more than a debilitating revolving door.

Community justice targets high-impact areas for another reason: these are where the problems are and where any progress made by community justice has the most payoff. A 10 percent reduction in crime in a neighborhood that has 10 crimes a year will barely be felt; but a similar impact in a high-crime location with, say, 1,000 crimes each year, will be a major improvement in the life of the community. This is the reason these areas are called high impact – the potential for impact by purposefully tailored strategies is much, much higher in these locations than in other areas in which problems are less severe.

Thus, community justice can be thought of as a broad strategy that includes the following priorities:

1   Community justice selects high-impact locations – places where there is a concentration of crime and criminal justice activity – for special strategies designed to improve the quality of community life, especially by promoting public safety.
2   Community justice approaches its tasks in these areas by working to strengthen the capacity of informal systems of social control: families, neighborhood groups, friends, and social supports. This means that instead of adopting the usual reactive strategy of merely responding to criminal cases as they occur, community justice undertakes a proactive strategy designed to work in partnership with these informal social control sources to strengthen the foundation for public safety.
3   In order to strengthen community capacity, community justice initiatives develop partnerships with residents, businesses, and other social services to coordinate the way public safety problems are addressed.

Community justice, therefore, is both a strategy and a philosophy. As a strategy, community justice broadens the responsibility of traditional criminal justice agencies to make room for partnerships with various citizen groups and other service providers so that a more comprehensive level of activity is sustained in the high-impact areas. Strategies of community justice are directed to deal with criminal events and to address the informal social control deficits that make crime possible. As a philosophy, community justice seeks to be evaluated for the way it responds to criminal events or even problems of public safety. It also accepts responsibility for helping to improve the quality of life and building social capital in the locations where community justice is most needed. Community justice brings important notions of social justice to the criminal justice agenda.

Criminal justice and social justice

Modern philosophers make an important distinction between criminal justice and social justice. Because both involve notions of justice, they are each based on the existence of a fair set of rules for how people treat each other and how citizens are treated by their government. Criminal justice is a type of "negative" justice. It is concerned with the way a society allocates undesirable experiences to its members. The study of criminal justice is the study of the rules, procedures, and practices under which citizens experience the application of a criminal label and the imposition of a criminal sanction. Criminal labels and criminal sanctions are considered just when they are imposed upon the guilty, but only when imposed within the rules of substantive and procedural due process.

By contrast, social justice is concerned with the distribution of "good" things within a society: opportunities for advancement, personal wealth, and other assets such as health care, housing, and basic goods of life. In a socially just society these benefits are provided by a fair set of rules and are applied to everyone equally.

Criminal justice and social justice, then, are both concerned with what people "deserve." Criminal justice is a set of institutions and procedures for determining which people deserve to be sanctioned because of their wrongdoing and what kind of sanctions they deserve to receive. Social justice is the set of rules by which people get the good things they deserve as a consequence of their talents and by the fruits of their efforts.

To a degree, criminal justice and social justice can be seen as flip sides of the same coin. When a person does something wrong, criminal justice ensures that the person gets the kind of punishment that goes with wrongful behavior. When a person's actions are meritorious – working hard and contributing to society – social justice requires that the person enjoy the benefits of having lived that way. We say that criminal justice is flawed when a person can break the law without suffering the consequences. Yet we also recognize that social justice is lacking when people are unable to get ahead, no matter how hard they might work or how much they might "play by the rules," because the cards are stacked against them.

Although perfect criminal and social justice is a laudable desire, we live in a society with well-known flaws in its criminal and social justice systems. Regarding criminal justice, we are troubled that sometimes innocent people are convicted of crimes and the guilty go free. In terms of social justice, some groups face unfair disadvantages that make it hard to succeed because of an uneven playing field. Both types of injustice make us ask hard questions about the fairness of criminal and social justice. We have a very strong cultural expectation that people should realize the consequences of their actions so that both those who break the rules and those who work hard and play by the rules get what they deserve.

Recently, we have come to see that criminal justice and social justice are related. The most obvious relationship is that places where people face the toughest odds against living out the American Dream are also the places where there is the most criminality. Crime and disadvantage are mutually reinforcing aspects of community life. The existence of disadvantage, in the form of an inadequate labor market, failing schools, and impoverished households, creates the foundation for drug markets and other criminal enterprise. At the same time, the existence of criminal activity makes neighborhoods less desirable places for people to live and for businesses to flourish, with the result that disadvantage becomes even more ingrained in these areas, and the people who try to live and work in these places find it harder to build successful lives.

The fact that social injustice and crime reinforce one another in high-impact areas has provided one of the main incentives for the development of community justice strategies with an objective of reducing crime, as well as the social injustices that accompany high rates of crime. Community justice brings together the two concepts of criminal justice and social justice to build a response to crime that takes both ideas into account. Community justice is a strategy of criminal justice because it is concerned with the problems that contribute to and result from crime. Yet the essence of community justice as a strategy is to strengthen the capacity of places that are hard-hit by crime; in that sense, community justice has a concern for broader matters of social justice.

The marriage of criminal justice and social justice is most evident in the way community justice approaches local areas with an eye toward building social capital. The aim of community justice is not merely to process criminal cases but to restore order, strengthen community cohesion, repair the damage from crime, and build partnerships that nurture a more beneficial community life. Taken together, these capacities represent social capital, which enables communities to act in defense of their interests and to pursue collective goals. The marriage of criminal justice and social justice is most evident in the way community justice approaches local areas with an eye toward building social capital. The aim of community justice is not merely to process criminal cases but to restore order, strengthen community cohesion, repair the damage from crime, and build partnerships that nurture a more beneficial community life. Taken together, these capacities represent social capital, which enable communities to act in defense of their interests and to pursue collective goals.

Social capital refers to the social networks that persons establish to solve common problems. These networks involve the development of trust and reciprocal relationships to achieve the attainment of goals. Putnam (2000) discusses the collective value of these networks which involves getting to know persons of influence. Also important in these networks is the idea of norms of reciprocity which means that persons do things for each other with the understanding that the favor will be returned sometime in the future, possibly by a different person or group. These acts create a connectedness that creates a bond and ensures that necessary acts are done to move the relationship in a positive direction.

Putnam (2000) also proposes two other important concepts in social capital networks are bonding social capital and bridging social capital. Bonding social capital binds people who are similar closer together and reinforces the norms of reciprocity and solidarity. Bridging social capital is a bit trickier because it closes the gap between groups that are not alike. It involves groups learning about the differences that separate them from other groups and making a concerted effort to find common ground that can build trust. Once trust is established, norms of reciprocity and networks with collective value can be developed. Putnam argues that "bonding social capital constitutes a kind of sociological superglue, whereas bridging social capital provides a sociological WD-40" Putnam (2000: 23). Certainly, while bonding social capital is important in strengthening like groups living in high-impact areas, the development of bridging social capital will be the means by which meaningful resources and assistance may be brought to communities.

In more recent research on immigrant integration, Putnam (2007) discovered that the more diverse the community, the less its members trust each other or the government, and the less they participate in collective life or believe in their ability to change their plight. A surprising finding was that more diverse communities are less trusting, less cohesive, and less participative places to live. Putnam (2007: 149) said that in these locations people tend to "hunker down" and become less trusting not only of person who are not like them, but also less trusting of people who are like them. While this research addresses the issue of immigration, there are still potential lessons to be learned in examining current high-impact communities. Putnam's finding indicate that persons in their twenties are as likely as persons in their forties to be less trusting of others. As these communities grow and evolve, diversity will more than likely be one of their defining characteristics. The implication here is that as new generations become the dominant population in communities, caution must be taken to insure that isolation within the communities does not occur. Also, it cannot be assumed that younger persons will be more open toward tolerance of those who differ from them. Putnam's belief is that isolation can be prevented by helping people better understand that ethnic diversity can occur while people still identify themselves as American and part of the greater society. Such information can be helpful for external groups who provide service or resources to high-impact areas. This would let them know that there still may be some standoffishness and they might not be welcomed with open arms.

Another lesson that may be taken from this research is that it is conceivable that those who may be different may be offenders and former offenders who return to the community. When those who are labeled as offenders come into contact with law-abiding citizens the result is often the "hunkering down" that Putnam describes in the area of immigration. This hunkering down results in isolation and lack of support for offenders who are trying to rebuild their lives. Opportunities in employment, education, and the acquisition of necessary social skills dry up when the perception is that former offenders are the individuals looking for those resources. Using the prescriptions provided by Putnam to ease tensions in communities regarding immigration may be just as applicable for communities facing the return of offenders from prison or those placed on probation or parole.

Another philosophy that may apply toward addressing the building of social capital and relationships in communities is *communitarianism.* Communitarianism holds that there are some moral duties that we are required to do even if there is no immediate benefit realized. This belief is founded on the belief that it is vital that members of a community behave in ways that benefit the greater good and not in ways that benefit only the individual. Communitarians argue that having a community is vital for free individuals because it "backs them up against encroach-ment by the state and sustains morality by drawing on the gentle prodding of kin, friends, neighbors, and other community members, rather than building on government controls or fear of authorities" (Etzioni 1993: 15). This philosophy dovetails well with the idea that informal social control is the most effective method of crime prevention. Communitarianism appears to provide one roadmap for implementation of informal social control.

This philosophy encourages the development of behavioral standards that are morally grounded and based on the public interest. One concern often raised when discussing morality is who sets the moral standards. Many communities fear that those in powerful positions would push their morality and cultural standards on the less powerful. Communitarians argue that these standards must be developed by members of the community and should be agreed upon by most of the people living in the community. After these standards are communicated to members of the community it is vital that most of the people abide by the standards most of the time in order to preserve the values. For these standards to take root and become part of the fabric of the neighborhood, reinforcing actions must occur. Communities can not only encourage moral behavior but they can also help those who struggle to find their way back onto the path. The moral principles can be important because they not only censure the unacceptable behavior they also sanction behaviors that help achieve the common good.

Communitarians realize that in many communities less emphasis has been placed on developing moral values and individualism has taken over as the guiding principle. They also realize that if members of a community begin to dialog more with each other they would tend to find many items of acceptable behavior on which they agree. Encouraging members of the community to abide by these agreed-upon principles would diminish the need for formal control mechanisms to control unacceptable behavior. This type of behavior would also contribute to the building of social networks that develop the ability to self-govern.

It is obvious that some communities are capable of developing a moral compass and implementing informal social controls to reinforce acceptable behaviors and some communities are not. Communities lacking the cohesion or structure to help themselves must receive a helping hand from elements of society that can bring resources to help make the change happen. These elements can include govern-mental agencies, nonprofit agencies, and even criminal justice agencies. Adopting a communitarian approach can still allow for individual identity but behaviors become less self-serving and more oriented toward strengthening the common good.

Community justice, therefore, is not simply about a desire to increase public safety. It is also concerned with the quality of public life and efficacy of collective community action. Using crime as a fulcrum for leveraging social capital, community justice seeks to improve the life of the community through attacking the problems that surround public safety and ultimately undermine the capacity of entire social groups in a place to effect their well-being. Criminal justice strate-gies are typically individual and negative: they remove residents, one by one, from their everyday lives and impose negative, undesirable sanctions upon each.

Community justice gives attention to social justice, in that it is not merely negative and individual in its orientation. It seeks a positive, collective outcome as a response to crime: better communities. Because these aims are sought in the most disadvantaged areas of a jurisdiction, community justice is a vehicle of social justice.

The importance of "place"

Community justice begins with an important insight about contemporary life: places matter. It is easy, in our modern society with its technological infra-structure, to think that space has constricted in size and that everything today is global. It is true that the advent of such everyday technologies as the telephone, television, and especially the Internet, has reduced the importance of distance as a constraint on daily living. Today, a person can talk to someone living thousands of miles away, see events as they are happening halfway around the globe, and chat by email with someone who is sitting at home on the other side of the country. Distance is no longer the all-encompassing limitation it was a century ago.

To recognize that space is no longer so impassable does not mean that local environments are unimportant. Where a person lives turns out to be one of the most important aspects of what that person's life is like. This is true in developing countries, where a person is born into a community that may become that person's environment for an entire lifetime, but it is just as true in a thoroughly modern society such as the United States. In this country, people commonly move from place to place precisely because where a person lives has so much to do with what a person's life is like. America, one of the wealthiest nations in history, is extremely segregated in the layout of its living areas – its neighborhoods. The poor, espe-cially poor people of color, live in ghetto-like conditions where almost everyone shares a common dialect, dark skin, and poverty. Those with means move out to middle-class neighborhoods, where schools are better and expectations for life more optimistic. The affluent live in places where privilege dramatically expands the array of choices about how to spend their time and resources.

The place where a person lives greatly affects the schools that person's children attend, the leisure-time activities used to occupy time, the places the person eats, and so on. For the poor, who often lack easy access to transportation, there are other constraints. The neighborhood is the place that provides work opportunities (however meager) and is home to the friends that a person will have. Whatever is available in the form of recreation – and in poor areas, this is often very limited – will form the field of choices for spending free time. Shopping for groceries, clothes, and other amenities will be dominated by selections within walking distance. All this can be a bit easier in city settings, which is one reason that rural poor often migrate into dilapidated city areas.

Therefore, even though we live in the era of cell phones and Web searches, place matters. It sets the stage for how a person lives much of daily life and is especially important for those who lack the resources to leave their surround-ings easily.

What is community?

In this book, we will commonly use the terms *community* and *neighborhood*. What do these words mean? Are they interchangeable? Do they have specific meanings we should keep in mind?

Much has been written in the attempt to define *community*, and there are numerous interpretations of the word *neighborhood*. In this book, we will often use the terms interchangeably. But these terms are not strictly the same, and it is useful to make some distinctions in the meanings as applied to the idea of community justice.

The term *neighborhood* is almost always used to refer to a particular geographic area within a larger jurisdictional entity. Neighborhoods of this type develop a reputation and an identity, and residents come to say, "I live in so-and-so." But the boundaries for these sorts of neighborhoods are not always concrete. People sometimes disagree about where one particular neighborhood ends and another begins. Over time, the boundaries of neighborhoods are fluid, and areas that were thought to be inside one area come to be thought of as belonging to another. Despite this definitional murkiness and spatial fuzziness – the idea of the geographical neighborhood is one of the more standard and traditional ways we understand the places where we live and work: downtown, north side, the Heights, west side, Maple Hills, the valley, Riverside, and so on – we learn to designate meaningful areas within larger jurisdictions, name them, and understand them as coherent neighborhoods, even though locating the actual boundaries of those places can be problematic. For the most part, when we say "neighborhood," we mean a coherent area within a larger jurisdiction that most people see as different in some meaningful way from the areas surrounding it.

The term *community* can be used to indicate a neighborhood, but it usually has more personal significance. Community refers to people more than places. Even when the community is a neighborhood, the term connotes people who live there, as in the Elm Avenue community or the West Atlantic community. When we hear these phrases, we think not only of location, but also of the people who live (or work) in those places. When we say "community," we also can mean more than just a location. Sometimes, the term is used to refer to a group of people who share a common personal identity, regardless of where they live: the Ukrainian community or the African-American community. Used in this way, the term *community* designates a collection of people who see themselves as belonging together because of their backgrounds rather than their addresses. Another, broader use of the term refers to a group of people who share a common goal or set of interests. In this case, we would say that the student community, or the business community, has shared interests that, despite other differences, link them in the pursuit of collective goals.

Persons lacking in connections with other persons who share common interests may find themselves unable to pursue the goals they have established. Many times *life chances* affect the ability of persons to connect with others who share their interests. The concept of life chances is discussed in the next section of this chapter, but it can be an important factor in whether or not some persons can connect socially with groups outside of their physical environment. Life chances play an important role in battling a sense of hopelessness that may pervade communities whose residents do not see a way out of the cycle of poverty. The inability of persons to connect with others who share a common goal or interest may cause them to "fall between the cracks" when it comes to accessing needed services. These types of communities provide not only social support for members, but also advocate for their needs to those who may have the resources needed.

In the United States a vivid example of persons falling between the cracks occurred during Hurricane Katrina in 2005. As the effects of the storm inundated the city of New Orleans government officials began implementing an evaluation plan that was intended to take residents to safe places in and around the city. News reports from the scene showed that many residents living in the poorer sections of New Orleans were struggling to find their way to the locations where they could access the public transportation that was to take them to the designated safe places. It became obvious from watching televised news reports that a large number of persons had medical, physical, or transportation issues that prevented them from moving from their residences to designated pick-up points. While one can only speculate, it appears that had more people living in these areas been able to connect with external communities that shared common concerns there might have been more information available to the rescuers. Such information might have guided those in charge to modify rescue plans to accommodate the large numbers of persons who struggled to escape the fury of the hurricane. More importantly, the information possessed by social communities could have been used in authoring the rescue plan as it was written, thereby alleviating much of the panic that set in during evacuation efforts. Sadly, the true needs of high-impact communities are often not recognized until such a disaster occurs and emergency crews are already at work.

Community and neighborhood are related in America because people who share common backgrounds or collective purposes often live near each other. Patterns of immigration have led to areas of cities dominated by people of like ethnicity: Little Italy and Chinatown are good examples. People who immigrated to the United States may have found it easier and more comfortable to live in areas where others from their country had already settled and where their native language was widely understood and spoken. Alternatively, they may have been victims of discrimination, and these areas were the only places they were allowed to live. Whatever the reason, ethnic enclaves typically developed in the urban centers as a consequence of waves of immigration.

This has also been true of internal patterns of migration, especially with regard to African-Americans migrating northward from the South. These former slaves and offspring of former slaves came to America's Northern cities to find better work and to escape racism in the South; and when they arrived, they found them-selves moving into areas populated by other urban African-Americans. Again, this was a result of the dual pressures of housing discrimination and cultural comfort zones. Today in the Southwest, this pattern is repeating itself with regard to Spanish-speaking immigrants, legal and undocumented. Within cities, areas are coming to be dominated by those of Mexican descent, and these locations have the qualities of being both a neighborhood and a community.

It is important to stress that the neighborhood experiences of the last two centuries' waves of immigrants – Germans, Irish, Italians, Jews, and so on – emigrating here from Europe have not been the same as those of Blacks and Hispanics in the United States. Although many European immigrants have kept their identity as a community, they have been able to leave restrictive neighborhoods in a pattern of economically upward mobility. Over time, those whose parents were born outside the United States assimilated into neighborhoods where everyone's family did not hail from the same original location. Ethnic integration and even intermarriage have occurred, a process called the melting pot. However, people of color have not had the same experience. Many areas that were dominated by people of African descent nearly a century ago are still places where African-Americans outnumber others by 20 or more to 1. This concentration of poor, economically immobile Black families has been referred to as "the Urban Underclass" (Wilson 1980) and has not been broken down by the usual form of integration and assimilation that other ethnic groups experienced. Rather, it has experienced multiple generations of racial isolation from the mainstream and concentration in urban ghettos, without a reasonable expectation of any different circumstance. In the Southwest, the experience has not continued long enough to be determined the same, but there are troubling signs of a similar spatial concentration of Spanish-speaking poor in certain locations.

At the same time, communities of common interests, such as students or business owners, likewise suffer the effects of poverty, economic immobility, and social stigma. In socially isolated and economically disadvantaged districts, students endure run-down facilities, limited pedagogical resources, and an often disorderly and sometimes violent school environment. Similarly, local business owners experience fewer paying customers and lowered revenues and are unable to maintain their stores or provide quality products. When social isolation is coupled with economic disinvestments, we face a growing problem of concentrations of poor members of certain communities in certain neighborhoods, with little prospect of change.

How do neighborhoods affect community life?

This is a problem of deep significance to community justice. For people who find themselves born into these areas, place really does matter. There is diminished social mobility, economic viability, and personal possibility. Community justice, because of its concern for broader social justice, considers this aspect of poor places to be one of the most important issues that officials of justice must understand and confront. The place a person calls home affects the way a person lives.

Place and life chances

The most important way that a person's residence affects quality of life is through the way location influences later life chances. The term *life chances* refers to the possibilities people encounter in their lives and the likelihood that a person will be able to achieve personal and social goals. Being born to two, college-educated parents increases one's life chances, as does living in a wealthy family. On the other hand, being born into an impoverished, single-parent family or having a drug-addicted parent reduces one's life chances.

The idea of life chances is one way to keep the popular image of the American Dream honest. In this country, it is true that people who are born into deprived circumstances are free to work hard, apply themselves, and "make it." Some do. But people who start out with significant disadvantages find it hard to rise above them, and for most, there is little prospect of success in the upper ranges. The concept of life chances holds that most of the pivotal experiences of one's social and economic life – from getting into a college to landing a good first job; from developing social skills to meeting people who can help along the way – are established by the circumstances of one's birth.

One of these important circumstances is the place a person lives. "Bad" neighborhoods typically have a dearth of good choices: schools are usually below standard or worse, job prospects are limited, and positive youth activities are few. A short distance away, a "good" neighborhood will offer a youngster born there a good education, plenty of structured and safe leisure activities, and when the time is right, a convenient chance to make a little money while finishing an education. In the former area, kids, especially young males, find it easy to get involved in a gang, easy to start down the road of drugs and alcohol abuse, and easy to meet others who are involved in serious criminal activity; they find it hard to get reinforcement for keeping up in school, hard to envision a realistic road to a conventional life of success, and hard to develop the life skills that help a person succeed. In the good neighborhood, almost the exact reverse is true.

The way a person's place of residence influences that person's life chances challenges our sense of social justice. It does not seem fair that so much of a person's life is determined by the circumstances of birth, because where a person is born is a complete accident. Someone who happens to have a billionaire for a father will likely be wildly wealthy one day, but how can we say that this person's extreme wealth is deserved? Similarly, a child of a crack-addicted mother who grows up in homeless shelters will likely encounter the criminal justice system as a youth or even as a young adult; and even though we might all think that a criminal act requires a criminal justice response, it is hard to see how anyone could come from such circumstances unscathed.

Thus, place matters in life. It sets up a series of social circumstances that play out over time as a major part of a person's life story. If you disagree, try this exercise: Tell your life story to date. Make sure you try to do it in a way that helps explain why you are where you are and what is important about your life today. Then, notice that the significance of the role played by the circumstances of one's birth, including where you grew up and how you grew up there, is as determinative for everyone else as it is for you.

The concentration of crime and criminal justice

Neighborhoods differ dramatically in the degree to which they experience crime and criminal justice. This is part of what makes the concept of community justice so important, because each neighborhood will face a series of different issues regarding crime and justice. A one-size-fits-all style of criminal justice may work in some places but will probably not be effective everywhere.

To understand how crime and criminal justice concentrate, we can use geographical analyses that show spatial distribution of each. For example, when we compare crime rates among police precincts in Brooklyn to incarceration rates among police precincts, the variations are remarkable. The police precinct with the highest crime in Brooklyn has three times the amount of crime as the lowest. The difference in criminal justice activity is even more dramatic: the precinct with the highest incarceration rate has nine times more people per capita going to and from prison than the precinct with the lowest rate. These numbers tell a powerful story of what it must be like to live in these places. In the 73rd precinct, for example, crime is common, and a large proportion of residents – one in eight adult males – is removed for incarceration. By contrast, both crime and criminal justice are comparatively rare in other locations only a few blocks away. In the former, crime and criminal justice are an everyday part of life; elsewhere, crime and justice are remote concerns (Cadora and Swartz 2000).

Place and public safety

Recent scholarship has uncovered the importance of place as an element of public safety. This is most commonly understood through the idea of hot spots. For example, Lawrence Sherman (Sherman, Gartin, and Buerger 1989) showed that in the places he had studied, the majority of crimes were committed in concentration in very specific locations – for example, street corners, blocks, or addresses – which he called hot spots. Crime is far more likely to occur in hot spots than in the immediate surrounding areas. Later researchers have found that the pattern uncovered by Sherman is the norm. A small number of specific locations account for a disproportionate number of police calls for assistance and reports of criminal events.

What are hot spots like, and how do they become problem locations? The answer is complicated because there is not a particular formula for a place becoming a hot spot. Often, but not always, there is a late-night tavern nearby; usually, there are dark streets or hidden alleyways. A couple of abandoned buildings or a secluded empty lot can also become a hot spot. What almost all hot spots have in common is not so much their physical attributes but the fact that they are configured to allow criminals to engage in crime with relative ease, and they exist in locations or neighborhoods where crime is generally higher than elsewhere.

The discovery of the existence of hot spots has had enormous impact on strategies of policing, as we describe in Chapter 2. The effective police administrator can target policing strategies surrounding these hot spots in order to cool them down or curtail criminal activity altogether. The first step is to use crime mapping to identify the hot spot; second, an analysis is made of what makes crime occur at the location; and third, a strategy is developed to overcome the factors in those locations that lead to crime.

Crime mapping is traditionally seen as a tool utilized by the criminal justice system to track incidences of crime and disorder. New technology, such as geographic information systems (GIS), has allowed criminal justice agencies the ability to track "hot spots" of crime and plan how to address those crime issues. It is important to realize that mapping and spatial analysis can be used to assist governmental and social service agencies, as well, in tracking important demographic information which can be used to guide the administration of support programs in communities. The discussion about place cited the importance of this concept. Because those living in a certain location may experience poor schools, high unemployment, minimal transportation options, and poorly developed social networks, the need for diagnosing these problems gains more importance. GIS can provide a valuable tool for examining the health of communities.

For GIS to be successful and meaningful, spatial data is needed. In other words it is necessary that the data is tied to something that may serve as a physical marker for tracking purposes. Roads, school districts, city council districts, and buildings are just a few examples of spatial locations that could serve the purpose. Data collected by municipal or social service agencies can be overlaid onto maps of communities. The data selected for analysis is limited only by the creativity of the persons conducting the analysis. Any data that can be related to a spatial location can be mapped and a vivid picture of the infrastructure of the community can be developed. Advancements in newer GIS software have provided agencies with the ability to provide meaningful visual images to accompany written documents or statistical analyses. For information to be used properly it must be in a form that is understandable and GIS allows even those not formally educated in evaluation principles to more closely understand the problem.

Instead of looking solely at crime or offenders' residences, analysts can use non-crime data to paint a more accurate picture of the health and needs of a particular community. For example, mapping data about home ownership can tell a person if there is stability and resident investment in the community. Traditionally, persons living in rental housing do not become actively involved in neighborhoods because they have no tangible investment in the neighborhood. Neighborhood associations do not usually give attention to renters because they are not seen as having an investment in the neighborhood and there is a general opinion that should things in the neighborhood get worse, those who rent will just move instead of pitching in to help address the problem. Knowing the specific locations of rental properties and the demographics of the renters could assist neighborhood in reaching out to these residents. Many of the renters may bring social connections or knowledge to the neighborhood that could be tapped if they were invited to participate in the neighborhood operations.

Public works data could also be helpful for governmental and nonprofit agencies in determining where basic services are lacking or absent. When residents of a community are lacking basic services they are forced to spend their time and energy in obtaining those services. This leaves little time for networking with other neighbors or building social capital. When basic services can be provided to a community, residents are more likely to experience feelings of self-worth and increases in self-esteem should logically follow. Residents of high-impact areas tend toward feelings of hopelessness because they see few ways to get out of situation they are in. Overlaying public works data on crime and disorder data may provide a thorough insight into the relationships between these elements. If the relationship shows a correlation, actions other than intervention by the criminal justice system could move a community toward developing the ability to establish stronger informal social controls and strengthen the fabric of the neighborhood.

Having a wider array of information about a community would allow governmental and nonprofit entities to better focus resources and interventions to where they are needed most. If the ultimate goal is to make communities more self-sufficient and to strengthen informal social controls, a focused approach makes sense. Many in the field of criminal justice argue that this type of diagnosis is not part of the charge that society gives to the criminal justice system. The common wisdom is that the criminal justice system was created to address those who, for whatever reason, choose to violate the statutory laws. Implicit in this wisdom is that the role of criminal justice professionals is to apprehend criminals, investigate crimes, determine guilt or innocence, and incarcerate or otherwise supervise those found guilty of a violation of the law, nothing more. Such comments show the need for a change in thinking regarding the relationship between criminal justice professionals and communities as well as a reexamination of the role of criminal justice professions in the practice of crime prevention.

From a criminal justice perspective, the idea that crime concentrates in certain locations has led to new thinking about how to overcome crime there. Today, there are three main schools of thought about how to overcome problems of public safety that concentrate in certain areas: disorder, disorganization, and inadequate informal social control. These each make assumptions about the sources of crime and the circumstances that are thought to promote it. Although these models share some common themes, they are worth discussing separately in order to understand their core tenets.

Disorder models: broken windows

The "broken windows" theory is one of the most popular ideas about the way crime comes about in urban settings. First enunciated by James Q. Wilson and George Kelling (1982) in an article in the *Atlantic Monthly*, the broken windows argument sees a link between urban disorder and crime that involves a process of deterioration in those areas. Disorder, in the form of trash, unsupervised groups of young men and boys, noise, and the broken windows that gave the theory its name, creates an atmosphere that makes people think a place is not being "taken care of." It becomes a distasteful environment, so the tendency is for people to stay away from an area where disorder predominates by avoiding it, moving to a new area, or simply staying indoors. This urban disorder also sends a signal to those inclined to engage in crime that such an area will not be cared for, so deviant or even criminal activity will not be stopped or otherwise hindered.

These two impressions of disorderly public space combine to make crime much more likely. Law-abiding citizens feel uncomfortable in disordered areas and do not remain there long. Offenders, however, feel empowered in these locations, and when they engage in minor deviance that is seems to be allowed without formal controls, they interpret this as encouragement. Their deviance escalates from minor activity to ever more major crime. At least one study (Skogan 1992) of the relationship between disorder and crime has supported this pattern.

Advocates of the broken windows idea should be and are the most interested in the repair of urban disorder. William Bratton was one of the first practitioners of the broken windows idea. When commissioner of the New York City subway system in 1990, he decided to keep the subway cars clean of graffiti and quickly stopped any other disorder in the subway. His strategy proved very successful, and the New York subways vastly improved.

Surprisingly, however, the broken windows idea has led to a different emphasis among law enforcement officials: arresting and jailing minor offenders. Their reasoning is that these are the people who break the windows in the first place; these are the people who create disorder and whose minor deviance in public space leads, inevitably, to an escalation of deviance and more serious crime. Many New Yorkers believe that the aggressive arrest policies of the New York City Police Department under Commissioner Howard Safir have played a major role in the dropping crime rates, although many citizens have been troubled by aggressive police tactics that affect young men of color more than other groups. Studies of crime in New York suggest that this strategy may have had less to do with the drop in crime than did new police practices targeting problem locations (Silverman 1999) and changes in the socioeconomics and demographics of the city (Karmen 2001).

Disorganization models: systemic theory

The first important theory of crime and place, called social disorganization theory, was developed in the 1940s by Clifford Shaw and Henry McKay (1942). Shaw and McKay were concerned with explaining why certain neighborhoods in Chicago seemed to produce the most juvenile delinquents, year in and year out. They theorized that something about those places made it more likely for kids to become delinquent. Their analysis highlighted three sociological characteristics that seemed to matter most: poverty, ethnic heterogeneity, and mobility. When these attributes are present, the society in these places becomes "disorganized," and young people fail to become adequately socialized.

It is easy to see why these characteristics might matter. Poverty has always been a foundation for crime, one reason being that poor people have less stake in the status quo. Shaw and McKay argued that ethnic heterogeneity led to a situation in which there was less acceptance and agreement about the norms of conduct in the neighborhood, because different groups would have different values. Mobility out of the neighborhood meant that there are more people entering and soon leaving a place than there are long-term residents; consequently, people did not stay long enough to form attachments to others and thus help build the strong sense of social interdependence that made crime less desirable among neighbors who knew one another.

Recent studies assessing the usefulness of the Shaw and McKay approach have found evidence that cuts both ways: not only have poverty and mobility contributed to crime, but reciprocally, crime itself has come to perpetuate poverty and mobility. Poverty continues to be such an important cause of crime that some scholars (see Wilson 1980) have described an entrenched, inner-city poor so alienated from dominant economic and social forces that they form an urban underclass in which criminal activity becomes passed along intergenerationally and little hope exists for joining the economic mainstream. Ethnic heterogeneity is no longer thought to be as important as racial composition: areas where nearly 100 percent of the residents are African-Americans living in multigenerational poverty are typically areas with very high crime rates. These are places where most people find it hard to gather up the resources to leave, and so mobility tends not to be the issue it was in 1940. Recent work on coercive mobility (Clear and Rose 1999) suggests that the prison and jail system removes from and returns so many people to these areas that it has become the major source of a high rate of mobility in high-crime areas.

Social disorganization theorists seek strategies that "organize" neighborhoods by building social groups and creating political capacity. The idea is that a community that is organized can counter the forces of poverty, ethnic conflict, and outward mobility, which serve to promote disorganization in an area. Many studies have been conducted of community organization strategies (Moynihan 1969), including the famous Back of the Yards Project of Saul Alkinsky, which was designed to overcome the problems Shaw and McKay identified. So many community organization projects have been tried that it is impossible to summarize them in a few sentences; but it is fair to say that many of the community organization approaches end up in failure or attract strong resistance from city government, and getting the poorest communities to organize on their own behalf is very difficult.

Informal social control models: collective efficacy

A recent idea that borrows from both the disorder tradition and the social disorganization tradition is that of collective efficacy. Again, this work is based upon studies in Chicago by Robert Sampson and his colleagues (Sampson, Raudenbush, and Earls 1997), but it takes a different view of the way demographic forces work at the neighborhood level. The thesis of the collective efficacy idea is that crime is reduced when there are strong forces of informal social control at work in the neighborhood.

Informal social control comes from two sources: from families and other loved ones who exert controlling influences on the young people near to them; and from social groups and friendship networks that serve a similar function either in addition to or instead of families. Some neighborhoods have strong families or wide bonds of social relationships among adults and youth that lead to less criminal involvement by those youth. Other places have weak or "broken" families that exert inadequate control on the youth, and residents who neither know one another nor form social networks that have the capacity to support one another.

Thus, social networks – interpersonal relationships that people value and sustain – provide the ability for people to be collectively effective at producing control in the places they live. When social networks are weak or thin, there can be little collective efficacy. Research supports this view, finding that in neighborhoods where people know their neighbors and help each other, crime is lower regardless of poverty or racial composition (Sampson, Raudenbush, and Earls, 1997). Moreover, these studies find that disorder plays an insignificant role compared to that of collective efficacy.

Advocates of collective efficacy try to prevent crime by building social relationships in problem neighborhoods. They try to develop neighborhood organizations and centers that engage residents with one another, helping to develop social networks and strengthen social bonds. Unlike the externally directed community organizing that took place under the social disorganization model, which was aimed at organizing to get money and resources from city government, collective efficacy strategies try to build strength from within by forming groups that attend to neighborhood matters.

Box 1.1 Ivanhoe case study

In early 1992, the Kansas City, Missouri Police Department received a "Weed and Seed" grant from the United States Department of Justice. The Weed and Seed program is best described as follows:

The U.S. Department of Justice's Weed and Seed program was developed to demonstrate an innovative and comprehensive approach to law enforcement and community revitalization, and to prevent and control violent crime, drug abuse, and gang activity in target areas. The program, initiated in 1991, attempts to weed out violent crime, gang activity, and drug use and trafficking in target areas, and then seed the target area by restoring the neighborhood through social and economic revitalization. Weed and Seed has three objectives: (1) develop a comprehensive, multi-agency strategy to control and prevent violent crime, drug trafficking, and drug-related crime in target neighborhoods; (2) coordinate and integrate existing and new initiatives to concentrate resources and maximize their impact on reducing and preventing violent crime, drug trafficking, and gang activity; and (3) mobilize community residents in the target areas to assist law enforcement in identifying and removing violent offenders and drug traffickers from the community and to assist other human service agencies in identifying and responding to service needs of the target area. To achieve these goals, Weed and Seed integrates law enforcement, community policing, prevention, intervention, treatment, and neighborhood restoration efforts." (National Weed and Seed Program US Department of Justice, Executive Office for Weed and Seed 1998)

After careful consideration of locations to implement the program, the Ivanhoe Neighborhood located within the Central Patrol Division (CPD) was selected. The one problem with the selection was that only one-half of the Ivanhoe neighborhood was physically located with the boundaries of the CPD. The southern portion was located within the boundaries of the Metro Patrol Division (MPD) and the grant parameters were specific to the northern half of the neighborhood only. While the MPD portion of the neighborhood was upset with not being part of the program, it was decided to move ahead because the northern portion best met the criteria for selection and, from an internal communications standpoint, it would be difficult for officers from different division to collaborate on the program.

The northern portion of Ivanhoe was entirely contained within patrol beat 144 and the crime statistics for that area showed a neighborhood racked by violent crime and drug dealing. There were large numbers of abandoned houses and the majority of the residents did not own the houses in which they lived. Drive-by shootings were a problem with a large increase in those offenses occurring in 1991. Other violent crime also flourished in beat 144 as well. Since Weed and Seed had just been launched only three sites were awarded the initial grants, New York City, Kansas City, and Seattle. Each location was free to design their own program based upon the problems occurring the target areas selected. In Kansas City, it was determined that to achieve a better long-term effect the program should be built upon the philosophy of Problem-Oriented Policing (POP). Lawrence Sherman of the University of Maryland was chosen to be the evaluator for the Kansas City program and he brought many resources from the university, including a full-time graduate assistant, to the program.

Because violent crime was such a problem in beat 144, the program team decided to target gun crime as the major focus of the program. Special patrols were sent out to try to get guns off of the street and the program became what was later known as the Kansas City Gun Experiment (Sherman, Shaw, and Rogan 1995). Police patrols were intensified with the "weeding" money and violent crime was lowered due to the effort.

The Ivanhoe Neighborhood Association was in place at the time the program began but it was struggling because resident involvement was lacking. Many who live in the neighborhood were concerned but they were frightened of the drug dealers and others who were involved in violent crime. During the duration of the program in beat 144 many stories of courageous residents standing up to the violent offenders emerged. Unfortunately, the funding for the program contained an abundance of "weed" money and almost nothing in "seed" money. The neighborhood leaders were unable to attract many interested investors and commercial development in the area was progressing very slowly. There was little money for low-interest loans for those who wished to improve their property and so the majority of the activity in the neighborhood was law enforcement related. At one point during the early stages of the program, President George H.W. Bush visited the neighborhood and had a meeting with a few of the longtime residents of the neighborhood. His visit was welcomed and highly publicized in the local media but it did not translate into any immediate "seed" money from the government.

The program did have positive results in the area of reduction of violent crime in beat 144. A portion of the program that did not show results immediately was the strengthening of the neighborhood association. There were committed residents who continued working to build a social network within the neighborhood and encourage economic development. In 1997, the neighborhood took an upward turn and began to build momentum in the creation of a governing council that began to steer the neighborhood in a positive direction. Around that time the police department extended the boundaries of CPD to Emmanuel Cleaver II Boulevard making the neighborhood part of only one patrol division.

Today the Ivanhoe Neighborhood Council is a thriving body that is very much self-governing. They established working committees in the areas of crime and safety, beautification, housing, and youth. Volunteers are utilized to operate the committees and the neighborhood is very much in control of their future. The neighborhood currently operates several programs for residents including youth sports, scouting, music, and restorative justice. The council is also active in economic development and jobs creation for residents. In addition, the council established a website that provides information for residents (www.incthrives.org).

In 2001 the Kauffman Foundation provided funding to hire staff, open an office, and begin the creation of a strategic plan. The neighborhood has continued and strengthened its partnership with the police department and a large number of drug houses have been closed. Approximately 200 lots that were placed in land trust have been returned to the neighborhood for rehabilitation and cleanliness campaigns have reduced the number of illegal dumping sites. The council now boasts a long list of partnership that include banks, law firms and Legal Aid of Western Missouri, government offices, religious foundations, and the University of Missouri-Kansas City. In the Fall of 2009, the council became a working partner in the Green Zone project that will rehabilitate homes to make them energy efficient using labor hired from within the neighborhood.

Place-based strategies and public safety goals

This discussion of theories of community life and community safety leads us to a discussion of action strategies to produce greater public safety at the neighborhood level. We discuss two general types of strategies: community-oriented criminal justice strategies and community change strategies.

Community-oriented strategies in criminal justice

Because this book is devoted to the idea of community justice as a criminal justice approach, the chapters that follow discuss in detail criminal justice strategies of public safety directed at the community level. But it is important to recognize how these community-oriented criminal justice strategies for public safety are different from the traditional criminal justice approach, and we discuss five such ways. The themes we list here will be developed and elaborated in the chapters that follow.

Places, not just cases

The most important way that criminal justice changes its strategic approach in a community justice orientation is by focusing on the attributes and circumstances of places more than on cases. Because various aspects of places – neighborhoods and communities – are so important to forming and maintaining public safety, it makes sense to focus on places in order to produce safety. This focus means that physical aspects of areas afflicted with high crime are studied and, when necessary, altered: vacant lots are renovated into small parks or playgrounds, dark streets are lit up at night, vacant buildings are torn down, streets that house open-air drug markets are closed off, and so forth. A concern for places also considers the importance of the people who live there. Residents are mobilized into action groups to provide support for one another and help reclaim public space. Child-care programs are created for unsupervised children. Job creation and placement programs are established for residents who need work. This, then, is a dual-track strategy: clean up the broken windows aspects of the neighborhood that tend to encourage criminal activity and organize residents so that more effective services can be provided to improve their prospects.

It is not easy or natural for criminal justice to change its level of focus from cases to places. Criminal events, and the people who are involved in them, are the inherent and, traditionally, only level to which the criminal justice system has attended. Police arrest suspects, prosecutors charge them, judges sentence them, and correctional officials supervise them. The expectation that all criminal justice action flows from criminal events and concerns itself with those events is deeply ingrained in traditional thinking. A concern for community-level issues does not replace the case-level action of criminal justice. After all, how individual criminal complaints are handled ultimately forms an important basis on which we evaluate criminal justice, even with a community focus. The concern for places, however, provides an additional target for criminal justice activity: to make neighborhoods and communities better places to live, work, and raise children.

Proactive, not reactive

By adding a concern for places, community-oriented criminal justice begins by becoming proactive rather than simply reactive. By proactive, we mean that community-oriented criminal justice tries to head off problems before they occur, particularly by identifying the causes of public safety problems and overcoming them.

A case-level orientation is by its nature reactive. Nothing can be done about a criminal complaint until a crime has occurred (or is alleged to have occurred). But community-level problems, especially those that are cyclical in nature, can be dealt with *before* they happen. That is one priority of a community safety agenda, which seeks both to handle events that damage public safety after they have occurred and to prevent their occurrence in the first place.

Just as the focus on places does not replace a focus on cases, the concern for proactive strategies does not eliminate the need for effective ways of reacting to criminal events that occur despite the proactive work. Criminal justice will always be evaluated, at least partly, on how well it responds to crimes that have occurred. The advent of community justice has meant that criminal justice is also evaluated on the extent to which criminal justice has been able to build strategies that prevent crime from occurring in the first place. This is especially true for both individual-level and community-level strategies.

Problem solving, not just blaming

Traditional criminal justice has been described as a "blaming" and "sanctioning" institution. Legal philosopher Andrew von Hirsch (1993) has pointed out that a criminal conviction requires both a finding of personal culpability and a finding of blameworthiness. In finding a person guilty of a crime, we hold not only that the person did the crime (culpability), but also that the person was wrong to have done it (blameworthiness). From this perspective, the "problem" of a crime is that a person appears to have committed one, and the "solution" is that the person needs to be punished.

Community-oriented criminal justice recognizes that a much broader view of the problem of crime is needed. How the crime affects the victim and the community is a potential problem that needs to be addressed; how the sanction might affect the offender and those close to that offender also matters. Just as significant is the need to gain an understanding of the problems that may have given rise to the crime, and then to try to address those as part of the prevention agenda of public safety.

Under a community-oriented criminal justice philosophy, it is quite reasonable to expect that wrongdoers will be found culpable and blamed for what they have done. It is also expected that the problems the crime has created for the community and the victim will be addressed, and the problems that a sanction will impose on those who are connected to the offender will be considered in determining how to sanction the offender. Another objective of the community justice orientation is to identify the problems in the community that make crime more likely to occur and to try to reduce their impact on community life. Building public safety is thus seen as a challenge to the system's problem-solving capacity at several levels.

Decentralization, not hierarchy

Because criminal justice so often places a premium on the use of authority in response to crime, there is a tendency for criminal justice organizations to have a hierarchical, authoritarian style: a chief district attorney to whom everyone else is an assistant, and a chief probation officer to whom everyone else is a deputy. The same kind of hierarchical structure is common in law enforcement and institutional corrections, with chain of command, operations manuals, and standard rules and procedures. In this kind of organization, authority is concentrated at the top, and discretion is limited at the bottom.

Community-oriented criminal justice strategies cannot operate within a rigid, hierarchical organizational culture. There are several reasons for this, but two are prominent. First, because these strategies tend to be oriented to particular places – neighborhoods – that exist within larger legal jurisdictions, it is necessary to decentralize leadership to those subjurisdictional levels. Criminal justice officials who are responsible for services delivered in particular neighborhoods have to have a certain autonomy to work in those neighborhoods. This autonomy is made necessary by the second reason for decentralization: neighborhoods are not all alike, so a degree of flexibility is needed to tailor activity to fit the particulars of the given neighborhood. Even though it is essential that the law give all citizens equal protection, the justice official working in a particular neighborhood must form relationships with residents and businesses there, develop problem-solving strategies that meet neighborhood needs, and give priority to certain issues that are most important in that neighborhood. A command structure, where every decision emanates from the very top of the organization, simply does not fit this philosophy of service delivery at the neighborhood level.

Fluid organizational boundaries, not fragmented organizational accountability

Traditional criminal justice organizations have a sense of their "turf" and work hard to protect it. Police do not like meddling by courts, prosecutors, or correctional officials; prosecutors are not concerned with how their work affects other parts of the system; and so forth. In classic organization theory, criminal justice organizations work hard to protect their boundaries from incursion by other organizations, even sister organizations serving the same constituency.

Community-oriented approaches form partnerships at the neighborhood level, and protecting organizational boundaries takes a backseat to the need to form and sustain cross-organizational strategies that produce public safety. Police and probation officers start to work together, and court services intermingle with traditional social services to provide a more comprehensive response to the problems arising from crime that are faced by victims, offenders, and other citizens. A premium is placed on effective coordination and cooperation, not effective separation.

Comprehensive community change initiatives

Some neighborhoods face multiple problems besides those of public safety, including housing, employment, child care, and health. Each of these problems is difficult on its own, but together they can create a daunting situation for those who want to improve the neighborhood's prospects. These issues are not easy to deal with because they are interconnected. People with poor health find it difficult to obtain or maintain good jobs, for example, and single mothers cannot easily work without child care.

In recent years, a new strategy for addressing the multidimensional aspects of poor communities has emerged, called the comprehensive community change (CCC). CCCs are systematic ways to confront the most entrenched problems communities face. They work by establishing a local development corporation that operates under legal authority to build approaches that confront the communities' most pressing problems. CCCs that take the form of neighborhood development corporations composed of resident staff and volunteers are referred to as local intermediaries. They are local in that they do not address problems outside the specific neighborhood boundaries within which they work. They are intermediaries in that they build partnerships among business, services, and institutions operating inside the neighborhood, and they seek grants and other funds to establish new services or augment existing services for the neighborhood area. Sometimes, they provide the services themselves, but other times they help bring together organizations and individuals who are in a position to provide the services themselves.

The starting place for CCCs, and their most successful area of work, has been housing. Working in neighborhoods where affordable housing was a real need, CCCs brought together investors, builders, and community groups to take advantage of federal tax credits and create a climate in which the renovation and construction of housing was more likely to succeed, both financially and socially. With a history of success in developing housing, CCCs have more recently turned their attention to creating jobs and improving services for children, especially health care for infants and expectant mothers.

Some people believe that a natural next step in this work is to undertake public safety concerns. This seems to be an obvious expansion of the CCC idea because the lessons learned by focusing on housing, employment, and youth fit well into the problems surrounding public safety. Following are three examples.

Political empowerment

Most people think of community organizing as a process by which residents band together and march on City Hall to demand new services, more resources, and attention for their political leadership. But one of the most important new lessons of the CCC movement has been that this form of confrontational organizing often does not work in the face of more insidious contemporary responses. As with any power-based confrontation, there is the ever present prospect of confronting a more powerful opponent. City Hall can overcome this sort of pressure in a number of ways: build a counter-pressure bloc, pit one neighborhood against another, or even buy off some of the leaders of the complaining group. The approach can even back-fire if the neighborhood comes to be seen as a political problem and no political actors want to be associated with it. City Hall may dig in its heels to teach the organ-izing group a lesson or to avoid having to face similar claims from other sources. Confrontational strategies, although sometimes unavoidable, rarely work out as intended and usually lead to a series of countermoves by opposing political forces.

Therefore, CCCs have developed a new understanding in recent years of what it means to be empowered and what empowerment requires. In these cases, rather than try to become powerful "against" some group, neighborhoods try to find a way to align themselves with interests that are strong, redirect the efforts of those interests toward mutually beneficial outcomes, and gain power through the coalition of inter-est groups. For example, a neighborhood that wants to renovate its schools will find that rather than march on City Hall, it will have more success by building a coopera-tive relationship among a firm that does renovation, a bank that wants to invest in improving the community, and a citizens' group willing to volunteer time working on the project. Rather than start a public outcry for more police protection – which, even if responded to positively, may not address the core issues and may produce other unintended consequences – the neighborhood will have more success by devel-oping relationships among a local parents' group, the police precinct leadership, and some of the local faith leaders. Today, grassroots approaches to organizing are increasingly employing more sophisticated ways to create power by bringing together groups who share a common interest in solving the underlying problem.

Economic development

Economic development is one of the best areas in which mutual interests can lead to empowerment. Investors know that places where employment is low, people are poor, and businesses are few – as in most high-crime areas – are places where it is very hard to establish a profitable business. At the same time, these locations represent untapped markets because there is such a dearth of business that the competition is slim. If a few of the problems these places face can be alleviated, they will become wide open as potential markets for new businesses, especially businesses that provide basic goods and services to local residents.

Seeing these areas as opportunities for economic development rather than as economic disasters opens up an entirely new conversation about them. Instead of avoiding them, businesses should be encouraged to form partnerships to help cultivate these changes. For example, construction firms that renovate existing structures stand to benefit as partners when investors open up new businesses in these areas, and employers stand to benefit when housing improvements lead to a more stable residential population. For all parties, providing an environment where there are fewer public safety problems is an essential foundation for economic expansion. Therefore, CCC initiatives have started fashioning a workable partnership among investors, housing interests, and renovators that can create a basis for economic improvement. Here again, it is the act of forging partnerships among those whose interests align that creates the empowerment needed to establish economic improvements.

Service sector improvements

In most areas, services are provided by separate agencies operating in a fragmented manner. In multiproblem areas, residents often are in contact with more than one service provider at a time: it is not uncommon for a single family to have different members involved with welfare, housing support, child care, and health care. Again, this is an area where forging coalitions of organizations whose interests align can help solve problems. In a kind of one-stop-service-center model in these communities, local organizations have been facilitating the creation of service consortiums that work together in the same building, enabling them to coordinate and strengthen their services to those in need. CCC initiatives often provide office space to these entities, and they channel residents to those comprehensive service centers.

Public safety organizations have observed these CCC-based strategies and have begun to see how these approaches can be adapted to the public safety agenda. They see, for example, the profound empowerment that occurs when private and public interests combine to create solutions to the problems that make public safety a priority. They can see how economic development and public safety go hand in hand, and making headway on one necessitates improvements in the other. They can also see how creating effective partnerships among justice service providers can increase the impact of those services. The CCC model, therefore, has lessons for those who would seek to promote community justice.

Evaluation of community justice initiatives

As criminal justice agencies begin to work more closely with communities to build informal social networks and human capital there will be a need to develop methods and standards for evaluation. Evaluation must be completed to know if projects or programs are having the desired effects. Knowing if goals and objectives are being met allows the participants to modify or continue a program depending on the results obtained during the evaluation.

Currently, criminal justice agencies utilize quantitative methods to determine effectiveness and these standards will not work in this new type of relationship development. Pure numbers will not provide a proper assessment of the work being done and governmental entities must be prepared to utilize broader, non-numerical methods of evaluation. One reason that numerically based evaluation has been so heavily utilized in criminal justice program evaluation is that it is easily done. Collection of numerically based data can be completed quickly and the results can be reported succinctly to the governing bodies that fund the criminal justice agencies. These funders may be local, state, or federal governments who also rely heavily on numerically based evaluations. Funding for criminal justice projects also come from external funding entities such as foundations or nonprofit organizations. Being able to report results to these funders in a numerically based evaluation is quick and usually can be done through in-house criminal justice agency elements. What criminal justice agencies may struggle with is the acceptance that community justice evaluation will best be completed with a combination of quantitative and qualitative methods which will necessitate evaluating criminal justice agencies' performance differently than it has been in the past.

The evaluation methods utilized will affect entities outside of the criminal justice system as well and it would be prudent to consult with these various groups prior to developing evaluation standards. As discussed earlier, a cookie-cutter approach to evaluation would be problematic because each community will have different needs and objectives. While criminal justice agencies may have the most difficulty adjusting to new evaluation criteria there may also be discomfort with other participants, especially those who may commit funding to programs or projects.

In most evaluation practice evaluators examine outputs, outcomes, impacts, and processes. Outputs are the goods or services that are produced by the program or project. They are usually easily measured but do not address the effect of the program or project. Outcomes are the effects of the interventions and can be measured. Measurements can provide the evaluator with information about what events or actions occurred as a result of the implementation of the program or project. Impacts are effects that are longer term and address broader issues beyond the specific program or project. Because impact evaluation depends more on longitudinal methods, they do not tend to provide the immediate feedback that outcome and impact evaluation can provide. Processes are the methods or mechanics used to implement and carry out the program or project. Evaluation of processes focuses on the efficiency issues relating to the program or project. In order to obtain a comprehensive evaluation of a program or project, all four evaluation methods should be utilized.

Thurman, Zhao, and Giacomazzi (2001) discuss several approaches to conducting evaluation. While their work primarily focuses on community policing, it provides some possible approaches for the development of evaluation in the area of community justice where more stakeholders will be involved in the interventions. The approaches are:

1   **Intuitive versus Scientific** Intuitive approaches depend upon the beliefs and perceptions of those evaluated. Often there is not a systematic method for collecting this data and the evaluation relies on perceptions from those who may not have all of the information necessary to draw an informed conclusion.
2   **Passive versus Active** Passive approaches rely on unsolicited information provided by the participant. While it is not wise to discard all unsolicited input, those receiving it must be aware that emotion or other personal agendas may drive the sharing of the information; therefore, it is imperative that this

information be carefully scrutinized. Active approaches are initiated by the evaluator and involve systematic collection of data. Such approaches usually contain more objective data that can be analyzed and generalized.

3   **Narrow versus Broad** Narrow approaches may only focus on one or two aspects of the program and exclude vital information needed for a proper program evaluation. Broad approaches tend to be more comprehensive and allow more information to be learned about the program.

4   **Summative versus Formative** Summative evaluations are concerned with the effectiveness of a program as it relates to specific program objectives. These evaluations will advise the evaluator if the program is meeting the specific goals. Formative approaches focus on gathering information that allows needed changes or modifications to the program. Information gathered from this approach will provide the evaluator with data about how to change or modify the program to meet the stated goals.

5   **Insiders versus Outsiders** Inside approaches utilize people working in or with the program to gather data and determine the findings. Outside approaches utilize independent persons to carry out data collection and analysis.

The Police Executive Research Forum recommends five perspectives in approaching the implementation of the philosophy of community policing. These approaches appear to be appropriate for community justice implementation as well and could be modified to meet the needs of involved constituents. The perspectives are deployment, community revitalization, problem solving, customer, and legitimacy.

The *deployment* perspective addresses how resources are moved into the community. In community policing this involves how officers are deployed to increase positive contacts with citizens. From a community justice approach this perspective would explain how necessary resources are deployed into a high-impact area. Because community justice involves more entities than criminal justice agencies, these resources would include governmental workers, nonprofits organization workers, and private sectors workers. By developing a deployment plan the resources needed can be identified more accurately and the deployment can be completed in an organized and efficient manner.

The *community revitalization* perspective focuses on neighborhood decay and eliminating the fear of crime. This perspective appears to be custom designed for a community justice approach since much of the work in high-impact areas entails addresses physical infrastructure problems and reducing opportunities for crime, which in turn lowers the fear of crime. In a community justice approach it could also involve the strengthening of social networks to build social capital.

The *problem-solving* perspective involves a focused approach to crime and disorder problems that involve both the police and the community in identifying a problem, analyzing its scope, developing a response, and assessing the effect of the response. Such a structured approach to problem solving in community justice could ensure that all constituents are working together in solving identified problems. Problem solving in community justice could also entail involve solving problems in issues outside of crime such as education, employment, transportation, and the physical infrastructure.

The *customer* perspective emphasizes the importance of listening to the needs of the citizens. This perspective is important because for community justice to be successful those in high-impact areas must become part of the process of identifying and solving problems affecting their lives. The paternalistic approach of telling citizens in high-impact areas what their problem is and how an outside element is going to fix it will not empower the residents to take charge of their community. The community justice efforts cannot be seen as something that is being done to residents but something that is done with residents.

The *legitimacy* perspective involves establishing the credibility of the police as a fair and equitable public service organization that works with all aspects of the community without favoring one element over another. In community justice such a perspective expands the earning of credibility to elements outside the criminal justice system. Governmental agencies, businesses, and nonprofit agencies would all need to ensure that their actions showed that their resources are dispensed equally. One obvious place where this credibility could be shown is in the area of economic development projects in high-impact areas. Economic development involves not only private sector investment but also government and nonprofit support.

Use of the above perspectives could be used to establish goals and objectives in the implementation of community justice initiatives. Data could then be collected via direct observation, focus groups, surveys, official records, and social and physical disorder inventories (Thurman, Zhao, and Giacomazzi 2001).

Community justice within traditional criminal justice functions

Community justice ideas are not new to the criminal justice system. The main criminal justice organizations – police, courts, and corrections – have been exploring various ways to improve community relevance with new programs and strategies, and these have formed the basis for a more comprehensive understanding of the possibility of community justice more broadly realized. The following discussion illustrates the ways some criminal justice agencies have been approaching community-oriented activity.

Police

In the mid-1980s, a small group of policing leaders and scholars convened at Harvard University's Kennedy School of Government to discuss the crisis facing American policing. This crisis was seen as stemming from lack of public confidence in the police and a long list of studies showing that the most commonly emphasized police strategies, from 911 calls to intensified patrol, had little effect on crime but carried severe, negative side effects, such as overemphasis of police response time and loss of public trust. This group was looking for a new paradigm for policing in America, and they developed the idea of community-oriented policing. Within a few years, this concept had swept across the country and soon became the standard operating theory, if not always the method, of police in America.

Along with the idea of community-oriented policing services came a renewed commitment to experimentation and innovation in police work. Police agencies became leaders in community organizing, developed new partnerships with businesses and civic organizations, and started trying to prevent the patterned recurrence of crime by using problem-solving methods rather than merely responding to crime with the traditional tools of investigation and arrest. In various departments around the country, place-based policing strategies began to pay off in reductions in crime: New York City's CompStat (comparative statistics), San Diego's Community Policing, and Boston's Operation Night Light (all of which are discussed in the chapters that follow) served as examples to the nation of what could be done to prevent crime if police put down their operations manuals and began working with the people and the problems that presented themselves in the neighborhoods they served.

Among the three arms of the criminal justice system – police, courts, and corrections – policing has undergone the most thorough philosophical reorientation toward community justice. There are two probable reasons for the prevalence of community justice ideas within policing. The first is that the inadequacies of criminal justice are most directly experienced by citizens as policing problems because the police are in more direct contact with community members. That visibility has led both to higher expectations and more available targets of praise and criticism. Second, the nature of policing has always been more oriented to geographical or place-based strategies and tactics. The fact that police departments have traditionally been organized according to more discrete geographical units than have the courts or corrections makes it easier to reorganize policing principles around the concerns of people in those places.

Courts

Because the court system operates on the basis of criminal law, which holds the US Constitution as its foremost document and applies across all the neighborhoods within a given jurisdiction, there is a tendency to keep the courts centralized and located in the downtown area of a city near the other buildings of city, county, and state government. At the same time, judges and lawyers are among the least popular public officials, and the court system has been facing a substantial reduction in public approval in recent years.

Three innovations have begun to bring the court system into a community-relevant framework. A few innovative prosecutors, notably Michael Shrunk in Multnomah County (Portland), Oregon, and Amy Klobuchar in Hennepin County (Minneapolis), Minnesota, experimented with the assignment of a deputy to a particular area of the city, which met with huge success. Citizens living in those areas began to rely upon these prosecutors for a new range of legal assistance, and the prosecutors took a new view of how the courts could serve this population. To mirror this change in prosecution, a few jurisdictions experimented with community-based defense services, and these were found to increase the impact of defender activity as well as to change the focus of the defender's work on cases. The third innovation was the establishment of community-based courts to develop special legal approaches and targeted services to address problems that were specific to particular communities.

Corrections

Correctional services have come slowly to the community-oriented movement in criminal justice. For the most part, the community-based idea for correctional services has been upheld within the probation, parole, and community corrections aspects of correctional work, where there is a tradition of thinking about community in carrying out correctional activity. Some of these changes have been cosmetic, but there has been a very recent surge of interest in ways that correctional systems can forge meaningful partnerships with citizens, private-sector interests, and other services in order to work better with clients. This has followed directly from a correctional interest in serving "places" better.

Institutional correctional administrators are now beginning to understand how important their work is for community quality of life. Every time an offender is removed from a community and sent to prison or jail, members of the community area are affected; and every time an ex-inmate returns to a community, that community is affected by what the prison has (or has not) done. Many people believe that the new frontier of correctional work lies in helping communities deal with the dual impacts of removal and return of residents.

Conclusion

It is important to remember that community justice is still an emerging set of experiments that range widely in scope and practice. Policymakers and practitioners are inventing new applications every day. In some cases, these applications will be rooted in the broken windows theory of neighborhood disorder. In others, they will seek to address community weaknesses ascribed by theories of social disorganization. And in still others, they will look to strengthen informal social control and build social capital in a neighborhood, which is identified as crucial to public safety in theories of collective efficacy. What holds these differing initiatives together as community justice and distinguishes them from other criminal justice innovations is that they are rooted in two basic assumptions: (1) there are critically important differences between communities – as between rich and poor – that suggest the need to tailor criminal justice strategies to the particular problems and priorities of each; and (2) the influence of stable families, good neighbors, effective social organizations, positive peers, and other informal networks of social control are the most important foundation for public safety.

The result is that regardless of their scope or the particular form that they take, community justice strategies will be characterized by a unique set of common concerns. They will focus on the circumstances of particular places, not just on individuals. They will be proactive in that they will look to head off problems before they occur, rather than respond to them only after they have become critical. They will be enacted through collaborations within the criminal justice system that cross agency boundaries, and collaborations outside the system with new community partners, such as community development corporations. In so doing, community justice will adopt new priorities associated with community well-being that are not strictly limited to immediate concerns of public safety, but which also include factors that contribute to the underlying causes of crime. In neighborhoods that remain entrenched in poverty, improved employment prospects, health care, and housing all become the shared concern of community actors and the criminal justice system.

Because community justice is concerned as much with social justice as with traditional criminal justice, it will measure its success in new terms. Whether the operations of the police, courts, or corrections are being considered, community justice will seek to answer this question: Have justice activities improved the community's well-being and the capacity of its residents to affect the quality of safety in their own neighborhood?

Suggested web resources

Social capital – www.bettertogether.org
Issues about community building – www.cpn.org
The Urban League – www.nul.org
Housing and Urban Development – www.hud.gov
Community Development Corporations – www.community-wealth.org
Community Development – www.ncadonline.org
Community Tool Box from the University of Kansas – http://communityhealth.ku.edu/ctb/about_the_ctb.shtml

References

Cadora, E. and Swartz, C., 2000. Community Justice Atlas. Center for Alternative Sentencing and Employment Services (CASES). Unpublished report.

Clear, T. R., and Rose, D. (1999) "When Neighbors Go to Jail: Impact on Attitudes about Formal and Informal Social Control," *National Institute of Justice Research in Brief* (July).

Ivanhoe Neighborhood Council. *Welcome Ivanhoe: A Thriving Community*, viewed November 2, 2009, http://www.incthrives.org/aboutus.phpto

Karmen, A. (2001) *New York Murder Mystery: The True Story behind the Crime Crash of the 1990s*. New York: New York University Press.

Moynihan, D. P. (1969) *Maximum Feasible Misunderstanding: Community Action in the War on Poverty*. New York: Free Press.

National Weed and Seed Program US Department of Justice, Executive Office for Weed and Seed (1998) *Federal Programs: National Weed and Seed Program – US Department of*

Justice, Executive Office for Weed and Seed, viewed October 12, 2009, http://ojjdp.ncjrs. gov/pubs/gun_violence/sect08-e.html; www.ojp.usdoj.gov/ccdo/ws/welcome.html

Police Executive Research Forum (1996) *Themes and Variations in Community Policing*. Washington, DC: Police Executive Research Forum.

Putnam, R. D. (2007) "*E Pluribus Unum*: Diversity and Community in the Twenty-first Century – The 2006 Johan Skytte Prize Lecture." *Scandinavian Political Studies* 30(2).

Sampson, R. J., Raudenbush S. W., and Earls, F. (1997) "Neighborhoods and Violent Crime: A Multilevel Study of Collective Efficacy," *Science* (August).

Shaw, C. R. and McKay, H. D. (1942) *Juvenile Delinquency in Urban Areas*. Chicago: University of Chicago Press.

Sherman, L. W., Gartin, P. R., and Buerger, M. E. (1989) "Hot Spots of Predatory Crime: Routine Activities and the Criminology of Place," *Criminology* 27, pp. 15–27.

Sherman, L. W., Shaw, J. W., and Rogan, D. P. (1995) The Kansas City Gun Experiment. National Institute of Justice: Research in Brief, January.

Silverman, E. (1999) *NYPD Battles Crime: Innovative Strategies in Policing*. Boston: Northeastern University Press.

Skogan, W. G. (1992) *Disorder and Decline: Crime and the Spiral of Decay in American Neighborhoods*. Berkeley and Los Angeles: University of California Press.

Thurman, Q., Zhao, J., and Giacomazzi, A. (2001) *Community Policing in a Community Era: An Introduction and Exploration*. Los Angeles: Roxbury Publishing Company.

von Hirsch, A. (1993) *Censure and Sanctions*. Oxford: Clarendon Press.

Wilson, J. Q. and Kelling, G. L. (1982) "Broken Windows," *Atlantic Monthly* 249(3), pp. 29–38.

Wilson, W. (1980) *The Declining Significance of Race: Blacks and Changing American Institutions*, 2nd ed., Chicago: University of Chicago Press.

Further reading

Social justice

Barber, B. (1984) *Strong Democracy: Participatory Politics for a New Age*. Berkeley: University of California Press. A description of a civic democratic model of politics.

Braithwaite, J. (1979) *Inequality, Crime, and Public Policy*. London: Routledge and Kegan Paul. A theory of the impact of social inequality on crime.

Pettit, P. (1997) *Republicanism: A Theory of Freedom and Government*. New York: Oxford University Press. An explication of the "republican theory" of just governance.

Rawls, J. (1971) *A Theory of Justice*. Cambridge, MA: Harvard University Press. The classic description of a democratic theory of the just society.

The concept of "place"

Anderson, E. (1991) *Streetwise: Race, Class, and Change in an Urban Community*. Chicago: University of Chicago Press. A description of how living in impoverished inner cities affects social capability and social life.

Bursick, R. J. and Grasmick, H. G. (1993) *Neighborhoods and Crime: The Dimensions of Effective Social Control*. New York: Lexington Books. A summary of the literature on social disorganization theory and an integration of that theory with systemic social control theory.

Logan, J. R. and Molotch, H. L. (1987) *Urban Fortunes: The Political Economy of Place*. Berkeley: University of California Press. A description of the analytical framework for thinking about "place."

Community

Etzioni, A. (1993) *The Spirit of Community: Rights, Responsibilities, and the Communitarian Agenda*. New York: Crown. An explanation and advocacy of the philosophy of communitarianism.

Gottdeiner, M. (1994) *The Social Production of Urban Space*, 2nd ed., Austin: University of Texas Press. How cities and local areas create space, and how space affects social life.

Putnam, R. (2000) *Bowling Alone*: *The Collapse of American Community*. New York: Simon & Schuster.

Broken windows theory

Kelling, G. L. and Coles, C. M. (1996) *Fixing Broken Windows: Restoring Order and Reducing Crime in Our Communities*. New York: Simon & Schuster. Description of broken windows theory and studies of broken windows policing in action.

Skogan, W. (1990) *Disorder and Decline: Crime and the Spiral of Decay in American Neighborhoods*. New York: Free Press. A study of the impact of disorder on crime in Chicago.

Taylor, R. B. (2001) *Breaking Away from Broken Windows: Baltimore Neighborhoods and the Nationwide Fight against Crime, Fear, and Decline*. Boulder, CO: Westview. A critical assessment of broken windows theory in Baltimore.

2   Policing and community justice

The police were in large part the first criminal justice agency to embrace the concepts of community justice, and so it is appropriate that we begin our discussion of the criminal justice functions with the police. The most obvious way that police serve as exemplars of community justice is in the deeply embedded community-oriented policing movement sweeping across America in the 1980s and 1990s. We will discuss this movement in more detail, but it is worth noting that community justice as a concept owes much of its momentum to the abundant success of community policing.

It is a bit of an understatement to say that community policing has swept the profession. Although the roots of community policing go back to at least the 1940s (Carter and Radelet 1998), a groundswell of support for the idea materialized in the 1980s, and by the turn of the twenty-first century, most urban (and many suburban and rural) police departments in the United States openly described themselves as using community-oriented principles. This shift to the community level represents an attempt to bring the police closer to the public they serve. Instead of simply responding to crimes, the community police officer builds relationships and partnerships with local businesses, organizations, residents, and social-service agencies; and the officer uses these relationships to better understand the needs of the community and better address local problems.

However, the community policing movement, important as it has been, is not the same as the community justice movement. The latter has derived a number of its most important lessons from the former, but the differences between the two are important to bear in mind. Community policing is both a comprehensive strategy of policing and a philosophy of law enforcement. Community justice, on the other hand, is a strategy and a philosophy of criminal justice. The recent experiences of police innovation in the United States have tested many of the most important community justice concepts in the police setting and have illustrated why community justice has become such a popular new idea.

In this chapter, we describe the police as an agency of community justice. We begin with a review of some of the issues that face modern police, and we show why community-oriented policing seemed such a valuable way to deal with those issues. We then provide a detailed description of the community- and problem-oriented policing approaches and assess their effectiveness. We conclude with a discussion of the current agenda for community-policing advocates.

A brief history of community policing

In the late 1800s and early 1900s, the police were under the control of those with political power – the police helped those who had power and punished those who opposed these powerful individuals. During this time, the public saw the police as corrupt and lawless. Eventually, after much public outcry, reformers of the 1920s managed to separate the police from political influence and created a professional, military-like administration system. In an effort to solve many of the problems of the past, and in order to appear more professional, the police became more distant from the public (Greene 2000; Kelling and Moore 1988).

Technological innovations also increased the rift between officers and the community. The use of automobiles severely decreased the number of neighborhood beat cops, and the widespread use of telephones and radios allowed residents to quickly and easily contact the police for assistance. The ease with which the police could be contacted significantly increased the number of calls-for-service, reducing the amount of time officers could spend on crime prevention and relationship building (in order to ensure public safety, police departments must respond to almost every call). The use of computers further increased the gap between officers and the community by increasing the importance of performance statistics and highlighting inferior policing, high-crime areas, crime trends, and response times. Instead of listening to public concerns, officers and managers became slaves to crime statistics (US Bureau of Justice Assistance 1994).

The distance between residents and police officers culminated in the social and political unrest of the 1960s – a time when members of both the civil rights movement and the antiwar movement actively participated in civil unrest (Palmiotto and Donahue 1995). During this time, the police were severely criticized for brutal behavior toward nonviolent protesters and blamed for instigating major riots through their aggressive, uncontrolled actions. These violent incidents, in addition to the well-publicized hostile relationship between minority communities and the police, sparked another set of reforms to improve the relationship between communities and police officers. After a few attempts to establish community policing had failed, the concept evolved and took root in the mid-1980s (Greene 2000). These topics will be expanded upon later in this chapter.

Policy and the community: a dual-track rationale

Community-oriented policing has two justifications that also apply to community justice in law enforcement. The two aims of community-oriented policing are better community relations and better crime prevention.

Better community relations are needed because police rely on the public in order to do their jobs, but there are several important impediments to good community relations. Some have to do with different images of the police by the public: citizens with advantaged social class tend to see the police in a very positive light; people who suffer significant social disadvantage do not have that same positive view. The problem is that the police mission is much more reliant upon the ability to sustain the confidence of the latter than the former, and therein lies a challenge: how to obtain and maintain positive interaction with citizens who may be predisposed to be suspicious of the police. But the problem is not only in the attitudes of citizens. Aspects of police culture and the police ethic also interfere with a capacity for positive relations – for example, when police develop cynicism about citizen groups and become negative about their work, and when the culture of the "thin blue line" prevents police from having confidence in citizens.

Better crime prevention relies on community-based practice. As we saw in the opening chapter, street crime concentrates in some locations more than others, and police therefore tend to be more active in these areas. However, if the policing approach is simply to be more active in response to crime – more investigations and more arrests – then the police will always be playing catch-up. If, on the other hand, the solution to high levels of crime is to take a proactive approach, there are more possibilities for public safety results. To do this, the police will have to change the way they act in the communities where the greatest police presence is called for.

The community relations rationale for community policing

To understand the need for a new orientation to policing, we must begin with a review of the main issues interfering with police effectiveness. We might be tempted to say offhand that the problem with police effectiveness is too many criminals. There is some truth to the idea that the sheer volume of criminal behavior makes police work a difficult assignment, but that discounts a profound and important truth: Police work faces a series of built-in problems that tend to frustrate the capacity of police to do their jobs well. This has to do with both the nature of the problem and the police themselves, at least in their traditional form.

We begin with a discussion of what we might call "the way things are," that is, certain factors in the job of policing serve to limit the way police can do their work. These are neither criticisms of the police nor complaints about the community. They are merely facts that set the stage for an understanding of the complexity of the public safety task. This discussion begins with a call for improved community relations as an essential first step in an improved police force and not simply as a desirable but less important goal. The importance of prioritizing community relations is explained by the nature of the policing job.

The police: essential services ensnared in quandary

In most places in the United States, the police and the hospital emergency room are the only public service organizations available twenty-four hours a day, seven days a week for citizens in crisis. Hospitals help us when we are sick or have a medical emergency; the police deal with us for almost everything else – and they often get involved in medical emergencies as well. Although we see police around us routinely, we encounter them only when our lives are not routine: when we are stopped for a traffic violation, experience some form of victimization, or face an emergency that requires an immediate response from someone in authority.

The facts that police are a full-time community service and that their work almost always comes into play when people are in trouble of some sort provide an essential foundation for understanding the police as a part of community justice. In a democracy, where citizens have personal rights and the police exercise carefully limited powers, it is impossible to understand the police and the community without acknowledging a quandary. The most important services provided by police usually take place in the context of somebody being in trouble or in some sort of crisis, so it is quite natural to expect the police to arrive with special powers to intercede. Yet the powers of the police to act are carefully circumscribed by democratic law and tradition, so the immediacy of the predicament is always tempered by the limitations placed on police authority. This often leads to disappointment, because the police will often feel constrained in the actions they can take and citizens will often fail to grasp those constraints.

In police–citizen encounters, the reverse problem can also occur. A police officer may interpret the facts of a situation as calling for serious or even urgent action, while the citizen feels intensely that his rights ought to constrain the actions taken by the police.

Small wonder that police often feel in that classic double bind, "damned-if-I-do, and damned-if-I-don't." In this situation, it is easy for police to become cynical, believing that nothing can be done to satisfy the public. It is equally likely that the public can become indignant, either objecting to an overreach of authority or disputing a seemingly lackadaisical approach.

This predicament of police–citizen encounters provides a powerful backdrop to our understanding of contemporary policing. It helps explain why the topic of policing receives such strong, often opposing, opinion: some people seem to despise the police, while others hold them in extremely high regard. A major defining characteristic for how people feel about the police can be race and age: people of color have lower opinions of the police than do Whites, and young people (especially those of color) have lower opinions than do older people, regardless of race (Sampson and Bartusch 1999). This makes sense, as these are the very people who are most likely to be stopped by the police. But it would be easy to exaggerate this problem, when the reality is more complex. Police consistently receive a more positive performance appraisal than do other sectors of the criminal justice system, even with all these built-in problems (US Bureau of Justice Statistics 2000).

How can it be that police are simultaneously so heavily criticized and also so deeply respected? The answer to this important question lies in an understanding of three aspects of contemporary policing. The police may be simultaneously thought of as a symbol of modern culture, a function of the legal system, and a function of power in society.

Police as a symbol of modern culture

The police represent social control, and they stand for social order. As the main coercive arm of the state, they also represent the power of the government. As a consequence, the police generate strong feelings among the public.

Many see the police as the symbol of a safe and secure society. This view holds that all law-abiding citizens share a common interest in safe streets, and the police are one of the main sources of safety. When police face constraints on their powers, those who see the police as the mechanism of social control often fear that disorder and criminality will follow. Those who hold the symbolic vision of the police as the agency of social control typically support a strong police presence, and they object to "civil liberties" views of the police that emphasize citizens' rights. When police are viewed in this fashion, it is easy to think of society as composed of "good guys" and "bad guys" – the police come from the former group and are asked to control the latter group.

Yet the police also symbolize the raw power of the state, and in a democracy, such power is uncomfortable to citizens. It is especially disturbing to members of minority groups who receive more attention from the police: African-Americans, Latinos, and the poor. To those who see the police as a symbol of power, the problem is not public safety but the way to place meaningful reins on that power. These people worry about police authority run amok, police action without controls. Because the most disadvantaged in our society are also the most likely to encounter police power used against them, this concern often arises along lines of social class and social status. People of color, especially young men, are very likely to be suspicious of police and less likely to accept their authority as legitimately exercised. There is a tendency to view the police as treating them and their neighborhoods differently than other people and locations.

It is easy to see how the symbolic importance of police carries community significance. The United States is today a residentially segregated society. Those who live in the residential areas occupied by dominant majorities see the police far more positively than those who live in poor, minority areas. Some of this opinion is related to the way the police treat people in those areas. In high-crime locations, suspects are numerous and suspicious situations routine; police often tend to take an aggressive stance, and the result is that many citizens feel deeply disrespected on account of the color of their skin. In the low-activity areas, police are less vigilant about crime, and citizens as a result feel under less scrutiny.

Thus, part of what determines the way citizens react to the police is how the police define the citizenry. When police see citizens as potential problems, those citizens often respond by seeing the police as a potentially unwelcome power in their lives. When police see citizens as "residents," those residents will see the police as a support system. The way in which police attitudes toward the public tend to create a public reaction was one of the original sources of the movement toward community policing.

Police as a function of the legal system

No matter what the police symbolize, they are first and foremost the initial stage of the criminal justice process. They take reports of criminal events, investigate suspicious situations, and make arrests. Few cases come into the criminal justice system without first encountering the police.

For this reason, police work has to be assessed on three different criteria: How do police actions affect willingness of citizens to report crimes? How do these actions encourage citizen cooperation with criminal investigations? And how effective are these strategies in identifying suspects accurately?

We would think that most law-abiding citizens would be anxious to cooperate with the police. But studies of police–citizen relations find that citizens who have had negative experiences with the police often become reluctant to assist the police in their investigations or report crimes to the police in the first place – even when they are the victims (Clear and Rose 1999). Indeed, in places where police–community relations are poor, citizens show a marked reluctance to report crimes and a strong hesitation to trust the police response to problems.

For police, this lack of cooperation has two sides. Any police officer who has worked in a poor neighborhood, especially a poor minority area, knows the level of mistrust and even antagonism that can permeate the attempt to do the work. It is frustrating, because the police point of view is that they are only trying to protect the law-abiding citizens from the "bad guys," and the lack of cooperation makes the work that much harder. Then again, not everyone is uncooperative. Some of the residents have an unabashed enthusiasm for the police to do their work, and this positive response by many highlights the difficult behavior of the others. It is easy for the police to view all the residents who express suspicion as somehow being aligned with "the bad element."

Nonetheless, when folks are reluctant to report crimes and when those who are surrounded by crime are disinclined to assist the police, the job of law enforcement, difficult enough without citizen recalcitrance, becomes more untenable. After a while, some police can develop an attitude toward the residents of these areas of "since they don't care, why should I?." Under these circumstances, the basic work of policing becomes more and more difficult. To protect themselves from an all-too-often unfriendly public, police adopt a first-choice style of indifference. When a victim or a citizen shows an appreciation for a police officer's effort, this can energize activity on behalf of that citizen, but others may come to see this as a kind of favoritism. In the end, the credibility of the criminal justice system suffers, as citizens lose confidence in it and the police become more cynical about their work.

Police as a function of power in society

In this context, the important distinction between authority and power can become blurred. *Authority* is the legitimate capacity to require compliance imbued in a role by law, standards, or custom. It is housed in the idea that some consensus of opinion exists that the person occupying a certain role ought to have a level of obedience to his or her directives, so long as they flow from legitimate exercise of duties within that role. Judges have authority in the courtroom, teachers in the classroom, supervisors in the workplace, and so on. So long as the person with authority is acting consistent with the expectations of the role, we expect voluntary compliance with the directives that emanate from the legitimate performance of that role. There is a certain expectation from all of us that people will *willingly* comply with the valid directives of a person with authority to give those directives.

Power, on the other hand, is the raw ability to compel compliance, regardless of the person's willingness to comply. When a person has power with regard to certain actions, it means that person can make others do what is wanted through some implied or actual coercive capacity. The ultimate source of power is the force of might – one who is stronger than another might be able to make that person do something, whether that person wants to or not – but power can also derive from the force of law or the force of group solidarity. For example, a police officer stops a person to ask a few questions, using authority, but then decides to detain that person, using the power of arrest.

The distinction between power and authority is important to bear in mind. Authority is a far more efficient means for getting a person to do something, since it works without any direct threat. Someone with the authority to ask simply does so, and on the basis of that recognized authority, the requested behavior follows. Power, by contrast, requires implied or demonstrated threat: we all know the implications of the statement "You are under arrest," and few of us will doubt the meaning of the order "Stop or I'll shoot," but it is the act of pulling out the handcuffs or revolver that communicates the meaning of the statement.

There is an important irony here. Authority, to work, is reliant on voluntary cooperation, whereas power can be exercised regardless of the other person's willingness to comply. In a very real sense, *authority is given* to the person exercising it by the person who has decided to comply, while *power is taken* by the person giving orders. Power, then, typically comes into play when authority is absent. Yet authority is absent not because of something missing from the police officer's role, but because of something missing in the citizen's response to that role. Authority exists because people voluntarily accept the dictates of the police.

Sometimes, of course, power and authority flow together, as when a judge oversees a courtroom, but usually there are important distinctions between them. Teachers, who hope to have broad authority in the classroom, in truth have limited power there. Police, who appreciate having broad authority over citizen conduct, exercise power only in ways that are very carefully constrained by law.

Thus, a police officer who is frustrated by a lack of authority cannot get authority through obtaining more power, even though this may seem to be the way to go. Authority is obtained by coming to be seen as legitimate in the eyes of the citizen, but obtaining power has almost nothing to do with the eyes of the citizen. Indeed, some might say that the more a person turns to power as the way to compel others compliance, the less everyone would expect that person to have (or even eventually obtain) authority. Often, the exercise of power comes at the expense of authority.

This is one reason why *the police culture* is such an important force in the work world of the police. The police culture is a set of informal standards and norms that develop among police officers and influence how they approach the job (Crank 2004). Volumes have been written about the origins and effects of police culture. The most common descriptions include the points we have made previously: police learn to approach the public with distrust and suspicion, expect that the public will not understand the job of policing, and view everyone as a potential problem (even dangerous). This cynical stance regarding the public is repeated when it comes to the criminal justice system, when the dominant view is some version of "the cops keep doing their job, but everyone else – from judges to probation officers – is soft on crime."

Three points must be emphasized here regarding the police culture. First, the police culture develops in response to the pressures of the job and the traditions of the department. Any problem with the police culture is much less an issue of "bad cops" than a human response to the difficulties inherent in police work. Second, police culture is not uniform across all departments and all divisions within departments. Important differences exist that make departments vary from deeply cynical and negative orientations to ones that are much less so, and these differences can even exist between, say, plainclothes detective units and the uniformed officers. Third, the police culture is not solely adverse in its effects. By adopting the informal norms of the police culture, newly hired police learn to support each other, avoid common mistakes, and deal with the pressures of the job.

But the police culture can, and often does, get in the way. Because it is typically cynical in its orientation, it tends to discount the value of authority and exalt the importance of power. Indeed, it is common for police to confuse the two, seeking an increase in formal power because of the weak potency of their authority. Most important, the dominant police culture puts the police officer at odds with the public. In high-activity areas, where public suspicions often match those of the officers, this is a recipe for alienation. Both the police and the citizens can come to feel that the officers in blue constitute an occupying army from an alien force, all parties at odds with one another, and little stake in common. What is often seen is a kind of standoff.

Two very strong values in the police culture are *control* and *dominion*. Control is a term that has unfavorable connotations. In police culture control refers more to the ability of the officer to ensure that responsibilities he or she is assigned are carried out in an orderly and effective manner. Officers must secure crime scenes and direct those who are not cooperating with the officer in the discharge of required duties. Control assists the officer in order maintenance within the assigned district or patrol area. Much of the emphasis on control comes from the basic academy training received by the recruit officer. Recruits are taught that they must take charge of all situations and that any sign of compromise or inaction can be seen as a sign of weakness which will be capitalized upon by lawbreakers and disorderly persons. Officers are taught that they must take control first and ask questions later. One difficulty that arises is that this style of behavior is reinforced because the officers encounter more confrontational situations than regular interactive situations. Officers become accustomed to acting in this manner and find it hard to adjust their controlling behavior in less threatening situation. This can be illustrated by a story once told by an elderly lady attending a community meeting. She said that an officer had arrived at her residence to take a report on a burglary that had occurred and during the interview he insisted that she be seated while he stood up to gather the information. The lady noted that the officer stood about 15 feet away from her at about a 45 degree angle. The officer had his feet also at a 45 degree angle with his gun side away from her. In relating the story to a commander attending the community meeting, the lady said that she felt the officer's questions were brusque and that it was obvious that the officer had no compassion for her victimization. For one who is familiar with police training, it is clear that the officer was in a "power stance." This stance allows the officer to respond quickly to any threat and sends a message that he or she is ready should an aggressive move be made. The disheartening elements of this story are that the officer, while doing nothing wrong, sent a message that he was in clear control of a situation where no threat was present. On the street, the officer's posture would probably not have been noticed; however, in a non-threatening, non-confrontational situation his posture sent a clear message that he was in charge and the communication was strained.

Dominion is a more passionate part of policing. Crank (2004) uses this term to describe what many would describe as territoriality. While people are territorial to some extent, dominion takes the territoriality one step further. When a person is territorial they are attentive to the property they own and they ensure that others do not damage or take their property. What is often missing in territoriality is the intensity of knowing very small details about the property or feeling a moral relationship to protect the property. Crank's term dominion refers to the belief of that officer that he or she has a personal ownership over the area of assignment. In dominion the officer knows as many physical details about the area as possible and is very attentive to the comings and goings of persons through the area. The type of behavior is often perceived unfavorably by residents living in the area and the behavior can lead to feelings that the police are an occupying force that is ruling their lives. Officers, on the other hand, see dominion as a moral responsibility they had toward protecting the area and the people who reside there. These differences in perception often lead to friction in the relationship between the police and the community, especially where the population is largely African-American or Hispanic.

While the degree of control an officer uses may be able to be moderated through the changing of training methods, dominion is something deeper. Because dominion is based to a degree on a relationship with the area to which the officer is assigned, it might be possible to modify its exercise into behavior that may be more constructive. If the officer is able to work with community members in a manner that encourages them to be as passionate about their community, social networks may be created that could lead a community toward more self-governance. One downside may be the creation of communities that infringe upon other persons' rights, but if the passion was implemented in a spirit such as communitarianism results could be positive. In any event, details of the community would be left to the residents of the community and that would be a positive move in strengthening community networking.

Problem-Based Learning (PBL) is a style of learning developed in medicals schools but recently this style has been incorporated into police training. The goal of PBL is to assist the student in solving unstructured problems. Educators have discovered that student may learn concepts well in the classroom but when they encounter a problem that does not conform to their knowledge base they are not sure how to address the problem. Since large numbers of problems that police officers encounter are messy and unstructured, PBL provides a method of helping officers pull together knowledge learned in training with experience on the job to better address the problems they confront. Proponents of PBL believe that critical thinking skills and problem-solving improves when learning is based on this model. For police officers a curriculum based upon PBL would involve examining case studies, participation in role-playing, and open dialogue about unstructured problems. Such training could be very helpful to officers who find themselves assigned to communities where they encounter daily problems that do not seem to be handled effectively through the use of traditional policing methods.

The community-oriented policing movement came about as an antidote to this sense of a police–citizen standoff. Leadership in policing saw the considerable negatives facing the police: problems with citizen relations, especially in the most disadvantaged communities most needing an effective police presence; difficulties with authority; and concerns about the impact of the police culture on police practices. All of this came together to suggest a need for change. Almost nobody was happy with the way that many communities regarded the police, and there was increasing criticism of the way the police regarded the communities they served. But even with this widespread and growing distress about the relationship between the police and the public, it took an unforeseen development to usher in the police–community era: a string of studies suggesting that the traditional approach was not working.

The criminal justice rationale for community policing

Improving police–community relations may be a central objective in the overall job of building a better police force, but there are other equally important reasons to change the relationship between the police and the community. Studies have shown that without good police–community relations, the police face extreme difficulties in carrying out their work. These studies were concerned with a variety of different topics in policing, but they led to a consistent general conclusion: the traditional manner of business in police work was not producing good results.

To understand this line of studies, it is important to summarize the traditional model of policing. In this approach, police see themselves as professional crime fighters concerned with the problem of serious felonies. This model has two important elements. With regard to citizens, police are expected to be detached and impartial, working "beat assignments," not communities or neighborhoods. With regard to crime, police are reactive and investigative, responding to criminal events based on their seriousness and building the evidence for criminal cases after crimes have been reported.

This professional model was the dominant model of policing from the early 1900s until the late 1960s. For most of this time, there was little questioning of the importance of the professional model, and police reforms took consistent patterns: more training, an emphasis on investigation technologies and crime-prevention hardware, and the adoption of paramilitary thinking about command, police deployment, and accountability. The idea was to downgrade the import-ance of duties that had little to do with crime (traffic, emergency services), allo-cate the most resources to the most serious crime, focus on rapid responses to criminal events, and maintain a visible, deterrent presence on the streets.

The first signs that this orientation might be in trouble came with the 1967 President's Commission on Law Enforcement and the Administration of Justice, which pointed with concern to the increasing problem of urban unrest, often taking the form of riots that began in the wake of some violent encounter between the police and a young person of color. The commission pointed out the urgent need for improvements in the way police dealt with the public, and it called for a reassessment of the way the police defined their responsibilities and provided services to the community.

There was also a serious concern about police performance. Crime and fear of crime were both increasing, while clearance rates for crimes and public confidence in the police were decreasing. Although this context was becoming less hospitable to the traditional policing model, a series of studies was leading some to conclude that the old emphasis on command policing simply did not provide adequate results.

The first, and most important, such study was the Kansas City Preventive Patrol Study (Walker 1992). This study employed a randomized field experiment to compare the effectiveness of standard policing patrol to proactive methods, in which two to three times as many police patrolled the streets, and to reactive methods, in which there was no police patrol and officers only responded to explicit calls for service. After these very different levels of police work had been compared for one year, the rates of crime in the areas were compared. The surpris-ing result found no significant difference in the rates of serious crime, fear of crime, attitudes toward the police, or even police response time.

This study threw contemporary police thinking for a loop. The study not only failed to confirm all the usual arguments about the need for more police, but questioned the very assumptions underlying those arguments. Traditional police thinking received a further jolt when studies of police response time – the amount of time it took the police to get to the scene of a crime after a citizen called for help – had little relationship to the probability of apprehending a suspect and was unrelated to citizen satisfaction with the police response. What really mattered was how long it took the police to get to the scene compared to what the citizen thought should happen (Carter and Radelet 1998).

Two other studies caused police to begin to rethink their strategies. A comparison of one-officer and two-officer patrol cars in San Diego tended to favor the use of single officers, both in terms of costs and citizen interactions. In addition, a series of studies of 911 calls for service found that by carefully explaining to citizens the priorities for calls and by helping citizens know how their case was going to be handled, the ascendancy of the 911 system over centrally managed priorities for services could be stemmed (Carter and Radelet 1998).

This string of studies, together with the continuing rise in crime and increasing popular alarm about public safety, led to a rethinking of what should be the best philosophy of policing. That rethinking was heavily influenced by foot-patrol studies in Flint, Michigan, and Newark, New Jersey; and fear-of-crime studies in Newark, New Jersey, and Houston, Texas. The foot-patrol studies found support for the idea that face-to-face interaction with citizens was an important part of citizen satisfaction with police, and that the closer cooperation between citizens and police that resulted may have contributed to safer streets. The fear-of-crime studies found that citizen–police interaction resulting from foot patrols helped reduce the overall level of fear. Together, these and other studies of the emerging idea of community-oriented police work began to call attention to the possibilities of change in policing.

Box 2.1 Community policing in Brooklyn

In 1984, the NYPD created a demonstration project named CPOP (Community Patrol Officer Program) in the 72nd precinct of Brooklyn. Through this program, 10 community patrol officers (CPOs) were assigned areas ranging from 16 to 60 square blocks. The CPOs set their own patrol times to maximize their effectiveness, and they were exempt from responding to 911 calls for service. In addition, each CPO kept a "beat book" with information on local issues and problems, strategies for solving the problems, and lists of community organizations. A plan for addressing neighborhood problems was outlined each month (Pate and Shtull 1994).

In 1990, the 72nd precinct was chosen to be a model precinct to test the feasibility of instigating a citywide community-policing initiative. The following goals of the model precinct project were stated (Pate and Shtull 1994: 387–9):

- Develop an organizational structure that facilitates the transition to community policing (increase staff; consolidate units; establish neighborhood beats).
- Develop an operational system that promotes and encourages the practice of community policing (improve communication among officers and develop monthly work plans).

- Develop an information system that would support community and problem-oriented policing (analyze crime "hot spots" create daily calls-for-service reports).
- Develop a system that would allocate the calls-for-service workload between foot patrol and motor patrol officers (low-priority calls will be routed to foot patrol officers whenever possible).
- Work with other departments to develop a comprehensive community policing model (detectives would be required to attend community meetings; introduce a fully staffed narcotics unit to the precinct that will work with foot officers).
- Develop a training program for all precinct personnel (teach concepts of community policing and problem-oriented policing).

Officers enjoyed the flexible hours and the opportunity to do something different and interact with community members. Interactions with residents in nonemergency situations made the job more interesting and more pleasant. Some officers did not want to join the unit because of the challenges of working outside in all types of weather, the feelings of being vulnerable without a partner, problems with responding to emergencies without a vehicle, the perceived lack of excitement, the lack of a clear reward structure, and uncertainties about the possibility of promotion (Pate and Shtull 1994).

Community policing

Community policing has three main sources of intellectual development. Robert C. Trojanowicz of Michigan State University was one of the more prominent scholars to write about the idea (Trojanowicz and Bucqueroux 1990). He founded the National Center for Community Policing, which advanced the ideas of the community-based (sometimes called neighborhood-based) model. According to Trojanowicz, community policing is a full-service policing model where the same officer regularly patrols the same area and forms partnerships with residents to solve problems. Mark Moore, of Harvard's Kennedy School of Government, initiated a series of Police Executive Seminars in the 1980s that clarified the theoretical and practical basis of community-oriented policing and then helped spread the innovation across the country. The most significant source of the change was the US Department of Justice Community-Oriented Policing Office that worked closely with the Police Executive Research Forum (PERF) to conduct workshops, studies, and seminars while publishing numerous reports on the concept.

Police scholars have identified three different types of community-oriented policing: community-building strategies, which attempt to strengthen community capacity; problem-oriented strategies, which deal with the causes of crime; and broken windows strategies, which focus on minor crimes and physical disorder. We discuss the current status of community policing using these main approaches as guides (Mastrofski, Worden, and Snipes 1995).

Community-building strategies

The most common form of community policing includes a range of tactics that help strengthen the community's own ability to reduce crime. Some of these are mundane and have proven to be of limited value, such as Neighborhood Watch or neighborhood meetings (Skogan 1992). Others are of more durable impact, such as victim-assistance programs, police-minority relations initiatives, and the long-standing Police Athletic League. Variously, each of these types of strategy is theorized to improve crime-prevention effectiveness in three ways.

First, the effect of increased day-to-day interaction between community residents and beat officers is thought to promote community-based "intelligence." That is, the more police talk to local businesses and other neighborhood residents, the more information they are able to obtain about crime and criminals in the area. Second, the same contacts are thought to provide another way to reduce crime when the flow of information is reversed. That is, when police publicize information about trouble spots or crime events, residents are more informed and able to act to protect themselves. Third, and perhaps most broad, is the belief that "police legitimacy" within the neighborhood is crucial to effective local crime prevention because citizens are more forthcoming with information regarding crimes and some residents act in more law-abiding ways (Sherman *et al.* 1996).

What these strategies have in common is their attempt to improve some aspect of community life by increasing interaction among residents or creating a standing relationship between the community and the police. Community building is an intuitively attractive idea, as the communities hardest hit by crime are also the very ones that most need development. But attempts to develop these communities also meet major obstacles. Skogan's studies of community policing in Chicago show that it is difficult to sustain community interest in developmental activity, and even police who are enthusiastic about the idea sometimes find themselves like fish out of water when it comes to community organizing (Skogan and Hartnett 1997).

These obstacles derive in part from the very premise of their goals. Hard-hit communities are the ones that struggle the most to make more time to meet after hours and increase their everyday obligations. Strategies that focus on building relationships with effective community networks suffer when those networks are weak or need to be developed. Thus, the communities most in need of assistance are also the least able to take advantage of this particular approach.

Criminal justice agencies must change from their current approach to working with communities. It is often difficult to convince police officers that their job entails more than just arresting offenders and putting them in jail. When discussion about forming relationships with members of the community is raised, the responses of police officers vary but it is not uncommon for one response to be "I'm not a social worker, I'm a cop." One approach that has been raised in helping officers better police their areas of assignment and form relationships is the medical model of policing. This approach combines the analytical, relational, and enforcement approaches that allow officers to be varied in their work.

Harpold (1996, 2000) identifies six types of neighborhoods:

1   Integral – have high levels of pride,
2   Parochial – have homogeneous values and cultures,
3   Diffuse – residents have much in common but rarely interact,
4   Stepping-stone – starter homes where residents begin their home owning experience,
5   Transitory – residents move frequently or have little in common with other residents which causes a lack of consensus and cohesion, and
6   Anomic – residents have accepted criminal victimization as a way of life.

By identifying these types of neighborhoods, Harpold helps police officers see more clearly how neighborhoods differ and why they cannot be policed with a cookie-cutter approach. In proposing the medical model of policing, Harpold argues, "Just as doctors can detect cancer early and prevent it from spreading, police can work in com-munities to influence the variables that threaten community pride and self-esteem. Early treatment can help the community from becoming ill" (Harpold 2000: 24). He sees the police as diagnosticians who can work with the residents to establish a course of treatment that addresses the specific problems encountered by neighborhoods.

In the medical model, the police officer is charged with learning about the neigh-borhood just like a physician would learn about a patient. For police officers this can be done through the use of sociodemographic data, comparative crime analysis, and community surveys and interviews. After gathering the necessary data about the neighborhood, the officers, just like physicians, may find that traditional as well as non-traditional methods are needed to combat the problems. Harpold believes that just as physicians may be required to use aggressive methods of treatment such as surgery or chemotherapy, the police may have to use aggressive methods such as arrest and search and seizure. He does caution that the police officer must be careful not to treat the symptoms and not the disease and such a mistake can be avoided by becoming intimately familiar with the neighborhood being treated.

Just as in medicine, Harpold uses some of the same terminology in discussing the implementation of the model. In *Intensive Care* there is a need for the intense application of services from governmental, public, and private entities. In *Preventive Medicine* crime prevention practices such as Crime Prevention through Environmental Design (CPTED) and neighborhood watch are used to strengthen immunity to crime. In *Health Education* the officer helps residents share respon-sibility for their own health and define boundaries for accepted behavior by residents. While the previously listed items pertain to the neighborhood, *Bedside Manner* pertains to the police. Just as the relationship between a patient and a physician is important, the relationship between the residents of a neighborhood and the police is equally important because for residents to follow the plan estab-lished a relationship with the police based on mutual respect must be established.

For police this means that everyone must be treated with courtesy and respect unless they show that they do not deserve it. To help officers implement this manner of thinking they should ask themselves, "How would I like to be treated?". From an organizational perspective, police managers may need to intentionally select officers who have a service-oriented approach to their job to participate in this type of policing. The final point, *Physician Heal Thyself*, addresses the need for police agencies to be healthy before they can treat neighborhoods. According to Harpold, this organizational health can be achieved through pride, self-esteem, quality leadership, and comprehensive training.

The medical model concept is certainly not flawless but it can be helpful in helping police agencies understand the need to be more holistic in policing neighborhoods. It may also help police agencies who have resisted community policing strategies feel more comfortable in adopting more progressive policing techniques. Community policing has taken a rap from police because of the perception that it is soft on crime and counter to the law enforcement mission of policing. The medical model includes traditional policing methods when necessary but also interactive approaches that address long-term problem solving. Many times police officers become frustrated because they attend neighborhood meetings where only a small number of residents attend. In these situations it is easy for officers, especially younger ones, to believe that it is not worth their efforts to work with the neighborhood if the neighborhood will not help itself. With that conviction it is easy for officers to revert to traditional law enforcement tactics to address crime and other problems. Connell, Miggans, and McGloin (2008) examined an officer-initiated community policing program in a suburban police department and found a significant reduction in violent and property crimes in the targeted area. In the study two interesting factors were noted that might account for the success of the project. The first is that the officers selected to work on the project had been selected based on their desire to be a part of the initiative and the second is that the community policing model was not implemented department wide, only in a single unit. These findings appear to be in concert with the ideas from the medical model which proposes careful selection of officers who will participate with the neighborhood in developing a prescription to address the problems facing the neighborhood

Problem-oriented strategies

Developed by Herman Goldstein (1991), problem-oriented policing (POP) strategies are based on the idea that crime emanates from particular, persistent circumstances that can be identified, documented, and then overcome through systematic action, and that police should be more thoughtful and innovative when dealing with neighborhood issues. The POP approach is very focused in its method, and although several problem-oriented techniques have been proposed, the SARA (Scan, Analyze, Respond, Assess) method is the most popular. Using SARA, the officer scans the community for problems, analyzes each problem in a systematic way, designs a specific response to each problem, and then assesses the usefulness and success rate of the response (Greene 2000).

For example, an officer might scan the community and identify drug dealing as the main problem. The officer then analyzes the locations of drug-related activities, the times of day these activities take place, the opinions and feelings of community residents and businesses, and the capacity of neighborhood organizations, social services, and religious institutions to aid in the development of a solution. After careful thought and planning, the officer might decide that the best response is increased foot patrols by officers and citizen groups in certain locations, along with improved street lighting in these areas. The officer might also decide to contact the landlords of the buildings where the drug dealers live or work and attempt to get the offenders evicted, or arrange to have surveillance cameras installed. Once the response has been implemented, the officer assesses the change in drug dealing and any changes in resident perceptions in order to see if the initiative worked.

One of the more successful problem-oriented strategies has been hot spots policing. This style of strategic policing is derived from the fact that a very small percentage of addresses in a jurisdiction account for a significantly disproportionate number of criminal events. These locations can be identified by mapping crimes, and strategies can be designed to ameliorate the problems that make these places more criminally involved. For example, a check-cashing store between two bars can become a problem, or a liquor store on a dark corner can invite crime. The hot spots model is also closely related to a school of crime prevention called situational crime prevention (Brantingham and Brantingham 1990), which is based on the idea that crimes occur when situations exist that make crime possible. Situational crime-prevention methods study the distribution of crime across time and space, with the aim of identifying the reasons why these two factors coincide so frequently.

Problem-solving methods seek policing tactics that are intelligence based. An elaborate version of intelligence-based policing is New York City's CompStat (comparative statistics) meetings. Credited by many as a major contributing factor in New York City's drop in crime (Silverman 1999), the CompStat process involves the spatial analysis and mapping of crime at the precinct level (precincts are approximately the size of a neighborhood), and a report on any increases in criminal activity and the ways the local precinct will deal with these increases.

> These meetings are an integral facet of a comprehensive interactive management strategy which enhances accountability while providing local commanders with considerable discretion and the resources necessary to properly manage their commands. It also ensures that they remain apprised of crime and quality of life conditions within their areas of responsibility, and that the Department's ten Crime and Quality of Life Strategies are fully implemented throughout the agency. The meetings serve as a forum in which precinct and other operational unit commanders communicate to the agency's top executives the problems they face while also sharing successful crime reduction tactics with other commanders. The process allows top executives to carefully monitor issues and activities within precincts and operational units, to evaluate

the skills and effectiveness of middle managers and to properly allocate the resources necessary to reduce crime and improve police performance.

(NYPD 2001)

It should be noted that the CompStat process, and any use of computer mapping to locate crime hot spots, does not, by itself, represent community policing. This technique must be used in conjunction with community partnerships and community-level problem solving in order to form a complete community-policing initiative. Also, any current community-policing initiative could significantly improve its crime-fighting capabilities through the use of spatial analysis – knowing where crimes occur is one of the most important pieces of information for police departments.

Broken windows strategies

One of the most influential new ideas in policing is the broken windows thesis (Wilson and Kelling 1982). We have described this thesis in detail elsewhere, but here we consider the implications of the concept for police practices. A detailed description of the broken windows philosophy of policing has been provided by one of its originators, George Kelling, along with Catherine Coles (1996). They describe the experiences of broken windows strategies in various locations of New York City, San Francisco, and elsewhere. In these locations, the broken windows idea has been credited with a reduction in crime and an increase in public order.

Because the broken window thesis holds that crime results from public disorder, the solution to crime is to use the police to create order. Under this assumption, the strategies are directed at people whose public behavior causes the general public to believe that order has disappeared: homeless are required to go to shelters or they are arrested; drunks are arrested and placed in jail; disorderly people – those playing loud music, drinking alcohol in public, or otherwise disturbing the peace – are required to stop or are arrested. In short, the power of arrest is used to enforce public order, especially by requiring these people to abide by public expectations for conduct. In some places, the emphasis on widespread "stop-and-frisk" tactics has led to accusations of racial profiling. In these accounts, it is not behavior alone that leads to police inquiry and action, but a combination of behavior and racial characteristics, which are said to fit a profile of prospective criminal offenders. The problems associated with accusations of racial profiling represent some of the civil rights limitations to crime-prevention techniques that depend too heavily on police intervention in the absence of citizen partnerships.

Another controversial form of community policing is evinced in broken windows policing as it has been implemented in New York City's "zero-tolerance" policing practices. The zero-tolerance method uses arrests of minor offenders – jaywalkers and those holding opened beer cans in public – as a means of quelling public disorder. While stopping a person for a public order violation, the police search and question the violator. Proponents claim that this routine questioning of public nuisance cases has resulted in large numbers of illegal weapons being seized and leads to the arrest of parolees who have absconded and others who are wanted on arrest warrants, and that the processing of these cases leads to a major reduction in crime. Critics of zero tolerance say that the rate of apprehension of serious offenders is actually very low (Karmen 2001) and so most of the stops turn out to be a form of harassment. Many observers credit zero-tolerance policies in New York City for the tragically deteriorating relationships between minority youth (especially males, who are the most likely to be stopped) and the police.

Box 2.2 Westside CAN case study

The Hispanic population in Kansas City, Missouri increased by 95 percent between 1990 and 2000 creating a problem of undocumented Hispanic men seeking employment in the city's Westside neighborhood. The Westside neighborhood is a heavily Hispanic area and the neighborhood noted an increase in crime and disorder with the increase of the undocumented men. Potential employers knew where to find the workers and a high amount of foot traffic and vehicle traffic was created as employers and workers converged upon the area. The residents and businesses in the area suffered and people would not patronize businesses on the Westside due to the disorderly behavior which included public urination, fighting, and drinking.

Residents had a sense that calling the police would not be helpful because there was a belief that the police would not take any action to stem the problem. Because the residents would not call the police to report the bothersome activity, there were low reports of crime in the area. When police crime analysts looked at the area they did not perceive any problems through their analysis and, as a result, officers were not informed of problems. After more analysis and conversation with residents, the police identified three groups of stakeholders involve in the problem:

1   area citizens and business;
2   documented and undocumented men willing to work; and
3   documented and undocumented men not willing to work.

It was also discovered that that the behavior of those in group 3 was problematic to those in groups 1 and 2.

Police attacked the problem through the traditional approach of patrol and arrests but then discovered that these tactics did not address the problem. Officers found that many of the men who were detained did not carry any form of identification and it was also difficult for officers to determine which men were willing to work and which men were not willing to work. The officers noted that there was a lack of facilities for those men who waited patiently for potential employers to contact them. Because of the lack of facilities, disorderly behavior often followed when the men became frustrated with each other. Jail did not affect the behavior of offenders because the arrested men were often released on signature bond only to return to the area and offend again. The Department of Homeland Security's Immigration and Enforcement (ICE) unit utilized sweeps that were also ineffective due to the lack of resources to address the problem meaningfully.

The police department talked with residents and business and discovered that both entities wanted the problem solved, but they wanted it done in a humane manner. Toward that end, the police department and the community researched day-labor issues across the United States and determined one solution might be to develop an environment where behavior could be monitored and controlled. A plan was formulated to address the environment and the Westside Community Action Network Center (CAN Center) was established. Working in partnership with the CAN Center, the police developed the goals, outline, and criteria for a Day Laborer Center (DLC). The officers knew that for the DLC to be successful the men must want to come to the new location, all workers must use the new DLC, and employers must pick up the workers at the DLC. Since the men in group 3 had no interest in such a center and continued acting in a disorderly manner, the officers worked with ICE to identify members of that group and take the appropriate enforcement action.

Soon it was discovered that there were too many men needing assistance and the search for a new location began. The CAN Center set forth criteria for what would be need at the new site. The criteria included the following: good access to major thoroughfares, space to accommodate 200 men, a nearby location to ease transition to the new center, a location far enough away from the liquor store to deter men from going back and resuming old habits, ample distance between the new center and existing businesses and residences, amenities such as showers, restrooms, laundry facilities, lockers, a kitchen, and meeting area, and, finally, rent of no more than $400 per month including utilities. After an exhaustive search, a suitable site was located. The site contained a machine shop that had been abandoned for over 15 years and the owner agreed to donate the building rent free for five years. Because the building had not been used for an extensive period of time, much renovation was required. A local construction company agreed to rehabilitate the building pro bono. Estimates by the CAN Center place the value of the donated materials and labor at approximately $150,000.

The opening of the new DLC brought immediate and noticeable results. The building that had stood abandoned was brought into code compliance, men no longer congregated on Southwest Boulevard, schoolchildren and neighbors no longer had to walk by large numbers of harassing men, the habitual offenders were removed from the area, the public sanitation issues were abated, prostitutes no longer gathered in the area, and business sales increased. The police also found benefits to the new center. They enjoyed increased neighborhood cooperation, additional time for district officers since they were not needed as often to make arrests for disorder issues, the creation of identification cards to help officers identify the men and establish emergency contacts, and a 50 percent decrease in calls for service in the area. For the men, benefits came in the form of increased responsibility and legitimate employment. Rule breakers were identified and turned in by the men and the men who were regular at the DLC provided cleaning and maintenance at the facility. In addition, when men could not find employment for the day they volunteered their service in the neighborhood assisting residents in a variety of tasks.

Community policing and community justice

Community-oriented policing services (COPS) have played a central role in the community justice movement. But community policing is not the same as community justice. The COPS movement in policing is, for the most part, particular to the traditional functions of law enforcement: investigation and arrest. Although some of the more elaborate community-policing methods move out of traditional police functions in attempting to prevent crime, community justice is a broad concept that applies not just to crime, but to the quality of life in the community. It also embraces the nonpolice functions of adjudication, sanctioning, and correcting – discussions that we attend to in the following two chapters.

Thus, although we may think of community policing as the bellwether for change that has set the stage for community justice, integration of community policing into the broader community justice agenda will require still more change in the way the police do their business, even within a community-oriented philosophy.

The formal training of police officers provides them with the rudimentary skills necessary to enforce the law and maintain order. Highly emphasized during the training is the need for officers to take control of the situations they encounter and establish a course of action that resolves any problems contained in the encounter. This often causes the officer to become an arbitrator, providing resolutions that may be less than acceptable to the parties involved in the issue. Little skill development occurs in negotiating and mediating with persons involved in a conflict of some sort.

It is important to understand the differences between arbitration and mediation because the terms are often used interchangeably. Arbitration is a process by which a neutral third party intervenes in a dispute, listens to both sides, and then through a reasoned process imposes a decision about what action should be taken to resolve the issue. Mediation, on the other hand, is a process where the neutral third party becomes a facilitator in resolving the dispute. The mediator allows each side to present their concerns and then he or she assists the disputants in developing their own solution to the problem. The obvious difference in the two methods is that the role of the neutral third party is consultative in mediation and authoritative in arbitration. Neither method will work in all situations so it is important for the neutral third party to be able diagnose the situation and determine the appropriate methods to address the problem at hand.

Police officers serving as mediators have become more accepted over the past decade, although it is still seen as being on the fringe of acceptable traditional police practice. One prominent argument against the practice is that it is too time consuming for patrol officers and causes calls for service to be delayed while officers attempt to mediate disputes. Rarely is mediation seen as a practice that will save time in the long run by possibly eliminating repeat calls for service and improving the cooperation between police officers and the citizens they serve. Cooper (1999) argues that neutrality by the patrol officer during mediation is not an impossible task. The officer is required to be an objective professional during the process if it is to be successful. Cooper believes that disputes that are appropriate for patrol officers to mediate include property disputes, vendor–customer disputes, landlord–tenant disputes, and boyfriend–girlfriend disputes. Patrol officers have also found mediation useful in disputes involving residents in a neighborhood. In many cases, officers can usually mediate neighborhood disagreements involving shared driveways, unruly children, and noisy residents. Officers who utilize mediation often report that the basic practices of mediation have made them better police officers overall because they listen more intently and ask more probing questions during interactions with citizens. They also report that those interactions are usually more positive because the citizens feel that the officers are engaged in helping them and not just going through the motions of handling a call for service.

As can be seen, mediation and its concomitant skills improve the performance of police officers in many aspects of their job. It is also important to recognize that the use of mediation improves the skills of community members. Community members who participate in mediation sessions learn how to listen more intently to each other when divergent viewpoints are presented. Cooper (1999) notes that disputes sometimes have two layers: the latent dispute and the manifest dispute. The latent, or underlying dispute, is often unspoken and has to be teased out during conversation. To do so takes time, patience, and good listening skills. Often disputants see the manifest, or obvious dispute, and fail to resolve the disagreement because they only address the surface behavior. Persons who have participated in or been trained in mediation skills know to look for the underlying issue that may be the real issue. After participants participate in mediation they learn that disputes can be solved through dialogue and that force is not necessary. The listening skills developed also help residents better understand concerns of the other residents and interpersonal skills are learned or fine-tuned. Development of these types of skills move the individual into the establishing of social networks and the results can be the acquisition of resources and services.

Some police departments have incorporated mediation into the citizen complaint process. Community members who may feel they were inappropriately treated by the police can elect to have their complaint mediated and a resolution acceptable to both the citizen and the officer can be crafted. The Office of Community Complaints for the Kansas City, Missouri Police Department implemented a complaint mediation program in 2000, and the feedback from both citizens and officers has been positive. One benefit of mediation is that the complaint is addressed and a resolution is developed. In many complaint investigations there is not enough evidence discovered to determine if the actions of the officer were inappropriate and the complaint is unsubstantiated. Such a determination leaves the citizen feeling that they were not valued and the officer feeling as if he or she has been unjustly accused. Resolution to the dispute in a timely and constructive manner can be beneficial for the police and community in building solid, trusting relationships. Again, the citizen can experience the process of expressing a concern, being heard, and engaging in a meaningful dialogue to address the concern. This type of process also makes the police more accountable to the citizens they serve and this accountability has been lacking in high-impact locations. Trust between the police and citizens can only be developed if there is respect on both sides and mediation provides a mechanism to build some of that trust.

Community policing is not a panacea. Although it has been one of the most important systematic changes in criminal justice in the last 100 years, it has also raised a series of questions about the functions of the police in modern society and the capacity of the police to accomplish those functions alone. As we see in the following chapters, the courts and corrections both face the same questions about an expanded mission that seeks to produce greater public safety through increasing community well-being.

Box 2.3 Levels of community policing

Greene (2000) provides an important summary of the types of changes brought about by community policing, as well as the expected outcomes as a result of these changes. This discussion serves as a useful framework for understanding both the potential effort needed for the development of a community-policing initiative and the potential rewards of such an initiative. The table below summarizes these levels and the expected outcomes.

Environmental level

At the environmental level the police form relationships and partnerships with local organizations, residents, social services, and businesses and focus on problem solving and crime reduction in an effort to reduce fear of crime and improve quality of life. The mobilization of the community to address crime-related issues is thought to increase the social bonds, communication, and trust between neighborhood members, thus improving community cohesion and increasing informal social control (formal social control being the police, and informal social control being community conflict resolution through non-police involvement). Also, when residents have more contact with police officers, and when police officers illustrate an investment in neighborhood quality of life, the residents feel safer and empowered (Greene 2000: 321–4).

Organizational level

At the organizational level, community policing affects how the department defines problems and solutions, and how the actual organization is structured, including the organizational attitude toward the police subculture and the selection and training of officers (for example, the hiring of more minority officers and language training for officers in minority communities). The organization must accept a new set of values for seeing the community as a partner and developing new problem-solving techniques to create a true community-policing initiative. This also includes changes in internal communication practices and information sharing among officers (Greene 2000: 322).

Individual level

Organizational-level changes must also make their way into the rank and file and be inculcated by each police officer if community policing is to succeed. Officers must develop new problem-solving techniques and learn to view the community as a partner in their crime-fighting activities. Also, crime prevention must become a higher priority for the officer. Job satisfaction should improve as the officer becomes more connected with the community, and the officer will have to use a greater range of interpersonal and problem-solving skills in his or her new role (Greene 2000: 323).

Level of anticipated changes community-policing intervention outcomes

Environmental	Form partnerships with local organizations and residents; increase public safety; improve social bonds	• Reduced crime and fear • Increased level of trust • More communication • Better problem solving

Organizational	Redefine department-wide problem-solving techniques; have officers adopt a new set of values, develop new internal communication practices	• Improved training • More diverse hiring practices • Improved internal communication • Improved analysis of problems • Change in information flow • New performance measures
Individual	Develop new problem-solving techniques and interpersonal skills; change view of the community role	• Increased job satisfaction • Increased performance • More attachment to community • Wider role in community

Source: Adapted from Greene (2000: 324)

Suggested web sources

The Center for Problem-Oriented Policing – www.popcenter.org
The Office of Community Oriented Policing Services (COPS) – www.cops.usdoj.gov
The International Association of Chiefs of Police – www.theiacp.org
Policing.com – your headquarters for community policing – www.policing.com
Police Society for Problem-Based Learning – www.pspbl.com

References

Brantingham, P. L. and Brantingham, P. J. (1990) "Situational Crime Prevention in Practice," *Canadian Journal of Criminology* 32(1), pp. 17–44.

Carter, D. L., and L. A. Radelet (1998) *The Police and the Community*. Upper Saddle River, NJ: Prentice-Hall.

Clear, T. R. and Rose, D. R. (1999) *When Neighbors Go to Jail: Impact on Attitudes about Formal and Informal Social Control*. Washington, DC: National Institute of Justice.

Cooper, C. (1999) *Mediation and Arbitration by Patrol Police Officers*. Lanham, MD: University Press of America.

Cornell, N., Miggans, K., and McGloin, J. M., 2008. "Can a Community Policing Initiative Reduce Serious Crime? A Local Evaluation," *Police Quarterly*, 11, pp. 127–150.

Crank, J. (2004) *Understanding Police Culture*. Cincinnati, OH: Anderson Publishing Company.

Goldstein, H. (1991) *Problem-Oriented Policing*. New York: McGraw Hill.

Greene, J. R. (2000) "Community Policing in America: Changing the nature, structure, and function of the police," in J. Horney (ed.) *Policies, Processes, and Decisions of the Criminal Justice System*. Vol. 3 of *Criminal Justice 2000*, pp. 299–370. Washington, DC: US Department of Justice.

Harpold, J. A. (1996) "A Community Doctoring: A Medical Analog to Community Policing," in J. T. Reese and R. M. Solomon (eds.) *Organizational Issues*, pp. 319–33. Quantico, VA: US Department of Justice, Federal Bureau of Investigation.

Harpold, J. A. (2000) "A Medical Model for Community Policing," *FBI Law Enforcement Bulletin*, June.

Karmen, A. (2001) *New York Murder Mystery: The True Story Behind the Crime Crash of the 1990s*. New York: University Press.

Kelling, G. L., and Coles, C. (1996) *Fixing Broken Windows: Restoring Order and Reducing Crime in our Communities*. New York: Free Press.

Kelling, G. L. and Moore, M. (1988) "From Political Reform to Community: The evolution of strategy of police," in J. R. Greene and S. Mastrofski (eds) *Community Policing: Rhetoric or Reality*. New York: Praeger.

Mastrofski, S. D., Worden, R. E., and Snipes, J. B. (1995) "Law Enforcement in a Time of Community Policing," *Criminology* 33 (November), pp. 539–63.

New York City, NY Police Department (1991) *NYPD: New York's Finest*, www.nyc.gov/html/nypd/html/chfdept/process.html

New York City, NY Police Department (2001) www.nyc.gov/html/nypd/html/chfdept/compstat-process.html.

Palmiotto, M. J. and Donahue, M. E. (1995) "Evaluating Community Policing: Problems and Prospects," *Police Studies* 18(2), pp. 33–53.

Pate, A. M. and Shtull, P. (1994) "Community Policing Grows in Brooklyn: An Inside View of the New York City Police Department's Model Precinct," *Crime and Delinquency* 40(3), pp. 348–410.

Sampson, R. J. and Bartusch, D. J. (1999) *Attitudes toward Crime, Police, and the Law: Individual and Neighborhood Differences*. Washington, DC: National Institute of Justice.

Sherman, L. W., Gottfredson, D., MacKenzie, D., Eck, J., Reuter P., and Bushway, S. (1996) *Preventing Crime: What Works, What Doesn't, What's Promising: A Report to the United States Congress*. Washington, DC: National Institute of Justice.

Silverman, E. (1999) *NYPD Battles Crime: Innovative Strategies in Policing*. Boston, MA: Northeastern University Press.

Skogan, W. G. (1992) *Disorder and Decline: Crime and the Spiral of Decay in American Neighborhoods*. Berkeley and Los Angeles: University of California Press.

Skogan, W. and Hartnett, S. (1997) *Community Policing, Chicago Style*. New York: Oxford University Press.

Trojanowicz, R. and Bucqueroux, B. (1990) *Community Policing: A Contemporary Perspective*. Cincinnati, OH: Anderson Publishing Company.

US Bureau of Justice Assistance (1994) *Understanding Community Policing: A Framework for Action*. Washington, DC: US Department of Justice, Office of Justice Assistance.

US Bureau of Justice Statistics (2000) *Sourcebook of Criminal Justice Statistics, Section 2: Public Attitudes toward Crime and Criminal Justice-Related Topics*. Washington, DC: US Department of Justice.

Walker, S. (1992) *The Police in America: An introduction*. New York: McGraw Hill College Division.

Wilson, J. Q. and Kelling, G. L. (1982) Broken Windows. *Atlantic Monthly* 249(3), pp. 29–38.

Further reading

Community-oriented policing

Greene, J. (1999) "Zero Tolerance: A Case Study of Police Policies and Practices in New York City," *Crime and Delinquency* 45(2), 171–87.

Kelling, G. and Bratton, W. P. (1993) *Implementing Community Policing: The Administrative Problem*. Washington, DC: National Institute of Justice. A prescription of ways to create and sustain community-oriented policing systems and cultures.

Nicholl, C. (1999) *Community Policing, Community Justice, and Restorative Justice: Exploring the Links for the Delivery of a Balanced Approach to Public Safety*. Washington, DC: US Department of Justice, Office of Community Oriented Policing Services.

Radelet, L. A. and Carter, D. (1994) *The Police and the Community*, 5th edn, Englewood Cliffs, NJ: Prentice-Hall. A comprehensive review of literature on community and police interactions.

Zhao, J. and Thurman, Q. (1997) "Community Policing: Where Are We Now?," *Crime and Delinquency* 43(3), pp. 345–57.

Problem-oriented policing

Bayley, D. H. (1994) *Police for the Future*. New York: Oxford University Press. A challenging prescription of the methods and philosophy of policing in the coming decades.

Goldstein, H. (1990) *Problem-Oriented Policing*. Philadelphia: Temple University Press. The classic description of problem-oriented police theory and practice.

Police culture

Repetto, T. (1978) *The Blue Parade*. New York: Free Press. Analyzes what it is like to be a police officer and the problems facing urban police reform.

Rubenstein, J. (1973) *City Police*. New York: Farrar, Straus & Giroux. The classic description of urban police culture.

Police authority and power

Bittner, E. (1990) *Aspects of Police Work*. Boston: Northeastern University Press. A summary of the literature of police behavior and the forces affecting police effectiveness.

Davis, K. C. (1969) *Discretionary Justice: A Preliminary Inquiry*. Baton Rouge: Louisiana University Press. The classic essay on police power and police discretion.

3   The courts and community justice

Of the three main divisions of the criminal justice system – police, courts, and corrections – the middle justice function, the courts, has the furthest conceptual distance to travel to become community oriented. As we shall see, one reason for this is that the natural subject matter of the courts is the problems in criminal cases, not the problems of difficult places. Another reason has to do with the way the courts work, processing defendants through what looks a bit like an impersonal assembly line of decisions, from charging to sentencing. And yet another has to do with the traditional values of detachment and impartiality in the courts, which tend to disconnect judges and lawyers from their clients and the communities in which they live.

Despite these impediments, the courts have been in recent years a setting for enthusiastic experimentation with community justice concepts and strategies. After decades in which change was very slow in the courts and traditional models of court processing remained virtually undisturbed by pervasive changes elsewhere in the system, courts have become a beacon for community justice thinking, especially with regard to the handling of vexing problems that seemed intractable under the usual methods, such as drug abuse or minor crime.

In this chapter, we explore the way the courts have embraced major concepts of community justice and particular strategies of community-oriented court practices. We will see that innovation in the courts has resulted in fundamental changes in the way the court system relates to citizens, including victims, offenders, and their families. As extensive as these changes have been, however, we will also see that some advocates call for even more far-reaching reform, and the courts have only barely begun to address the needs of multiproblem communities.

Criminal cases, communities, and courts

The subject matter of the criminal courts is criminal cases, not communities, and this has been one of the main practical and conceptual impediments to community justice in the courts. The focus on individual cases is completely understandable, as courts were established to deal solely with criminal cases. Each unit of the court's business, the criminal case, is defined by a complaint filed by the state against a defendant. What is at stake is the legal status of a defendant's conduct, and the efforts of the professional lawyers in the court triumvirate – prosecutor, defender, and judge – are designed to assess the legal consequences of the accused's actions. These key actors in the court system perform their functions in interaction with one another, without much direct activity by nonprofessionals. Courts are traditionally insulated from outside forces, and emphasis is given to creating an environment in which professionally trained lawyers can use their skills in a formal, solemn setting to create outcomes that are seen by the public as just.

We will discuss whether this view of the courts, as a formal, somber institution of deliberation about criminal accusations, is wholly accurate. Accurate or not, the image of an independent, detached judiciary has a hallowed place in American jurisprudence, and it has operated as a counterforce to community justice thinking. Whereas the traditional view of the courts is that they are stately and detached, community justice is seen as informal and involved. Whereas traditional court procedures are dominated by professionals with everyday citizens silent, except when asked to testify, community justice is open to the views of citizens and supplements the professional practice of the law with informal participation by people who are not lawyers.

Perhaps most important, whereas the traditional courts serve legal jurisdictions, such as states, districts, or municipalities, community justice devotes its attention to a particular location, such as a neighborhood, that is part of a legal jurisdiction. Courts give a high premium to the concept of equal justice under law, which means that every person within that legal jurisdiction is to be treated the same way by the court workers. Community justice accepts the foundational importance of the concept of equal justice, but sees within that idea a broad range of flexibility to tailor programs and legal strategies to fit the particular circumstances of communities affected by the law. Equal justice is important, but justice that addresses the needs of people most affected by the court system is seen as even more central to what the courts are called upon to do.

These two conceptual challenges have made it complicated for the court system to adopt community-oriented strategies. How can the courts shift their traditional focus on due process of law given to specific criminal cases so that they include a concern for the community-level impact of court case outcomes? Without violating well-established and profoundly important constitutional rights that have evolved over two centuries of litigation, how can the courts embrace a growing concern for the quality of life in the communities the courts serve? These are difficult questions. Our review of the current efforts to bring community-oriented ideas to the courts will show that today's court innovators are successfully creating strategies that embrace the new court's concerns without violating its traditional values. There is nowhere a perfect community justice court on which to model all community-based court innovation, but neither is there a perfect traditional court. What court reformers have been doing involves rebuilding court processes, procedures, and jurisdictions so that community-oriented values can emerge within the broader context of individual protections. In the end, courts still apply the law from a larger political jurisdiction to individual criminal cases, but community-oriented courts do this in a way that takes into account the need for community justice in the way these decisions are produced and carried out.

The two functions of criminal courts

Courts have two main responsibilities: they adjudicate disputes, and they determine the sanctions that will apply in cases that have been adjudicated. In each of these two areas, issues arise concerning two core values underlying the way the courts do their work: justice and rights. Justice issues are concerned with outcomes, asking the question "What results best fit the circumstances of the case?" Rights issues are concerned with the procedures used to determine the outcomes of cases, asking a different question, "What practices should be employed (or prohibited) in developing the outcome for the case?"

Table 3.1 illustrates the different rights and justice issues related to the two functions of the courts. As we see from the discussion that follows, the concern for rights and the criterion of justice each pose quite different challenges for community-oriented strategies of adjudication and sanctioning in the courts.

Adjudication of complaints

The first function of the criminal courts is to adjudicate a criminal complaint. The criminal complaint is a formal document, called an indictment or an information, filed by the prosecution accusing a citizen of violating the law. This document brings the case to the attention of the court. The criminal complaint alleges certain conduct in violation of the law, and it calls upon the defendant to answer the allegations. In the courtroom, the defendant answers those charges, and, if the defendant claims to be "not guilty," demands that the prosecution offer evidence in proof of the allegations.

One way of looking at the criminal complaint is that it brings about a dispute between the citizen and the state. (That is why criminal cases are referred to, for example, as *State v. Jones.*) At the technical level, the dispute is about the legal status of the defendant, whether the label "offender" may be applied to the

Table 3.1 Balancing concerns for rights vs. justice in the court

	Adjudication	*Sanctioning*
Rights	Concern that the defendant receives due process under the law and that the innocent are not mistakenly found guilty	Concern that the "punishment fit the crime" and is equally applied in like cases
Justice	Concern that the guilty are not mistakenly exonerated	Concern that sanctions take differing circumstances into account and are not counterproductive

defendant by virtue of conduct. In terms of practical implications, the dispute is about whether the defendant may be sanctioned for the alleged conduct. Before the person can be labeled an offender and prior to the imposition of punishment, guilt must be proven. The citizen's status must be shifted from "defendant" to "offender."

In adjudicating the dispute, the values of "justice" and "rights" play a powerful role. Two types of unjust outcomes are possible in adjudication. One occurs when an innocent person is mistakenly found guilty, the other when the case against a person who committed the crime is not proven, and the verdict is "not guilty." Although both values of rights and justice are important, the adjudication function seems to place a higher priority on rights, especially defendant's rights, than on justice. The Constitution gives the defendant the right to reject taking the witness stand and prevents the state from using evidence that has been obtained in violation of the defendant's rights. Legal traditions require that guilt be established "beyond a reasonable doubt."

The emphasis placed on rights is meant to make it difficult for the state to prove its case, and it suggests that when it comes to adjudication, not all forms of unjust outcomes are to be considered equal. This is illustrated by the commonly repeated aphorism, "Better for a hundred guilty men to go free than for one innocent to be convicted" (Justice Learned Hand).

Community justice advocates do not view the adjudication function as a contest. As a consequence, the community justice strategy tends to be less formal in its approach and tries to bring a concern for rights and a belief in outcomes that are just into a better balance. This poses one of the most difficult challenges for community justice as a strategy of the courts. America has a long-standing and immensely important tradition of individual rights as a starting point for adjudication of criminal complaints. How the courts can embrace a concern for community-oriented justice without discarding or depreciating the enormously important tradition of rights is, as we shall see, a significant challenge.

Sanctioning wrongdoers

For those who are found guilty, the courts must determine the appropriate sanction. The term *appropriate* is not easily defined, in practice, because a penal sanction that seems right to one person may seem too lenient or too severe to another. We all may want a court system that imposes penalties that fit the circumstances of the case, but there may be little agreement about the facts of the case that the penalty should be fitted to. Do the offender's personal characteristics matter? Which ones? Does it matter that the defendant is young, or intellectually limited, or poor, or a mother? What aspects of the crime itself are to be considered? Do we care if the offender was provoked? Does it matter if the way the crime occurred was particularly wanton?

When it comes to imposing a sanction, the concern for an outcome that is just rises in importance, and the prominence of rights is diminished. Of course, the offender's rights are still intact and may not be violated, but we recognize that the sanctioning process is mostly about selecting a penalty that fits the case. Whereas adjudication is about a process of law, sanctioning is about determining the right legal outcome of that process.

Among legal scholars there is some disagreement about the outcome the sanction ought to be tailored to achieve. An eloquent case can be made that the purpose of a sanction is primarily to punish, to impose a penalty that fits the seriousness of the crime (von Hirsch 1993). But equally persuasive arguments exist in favor of sanctions that rehabilitate (Cullen and Gendreau 1989) and incapacitate (Zedlewski 1987). With this kind of disagreement about the basic aims of a penal sanction, it is not surprising that people frequently disagree about the best penalty to impose upon a newly convicted offender.

In selecting a penalty, the conversation turns from rights to justice: What penalty fits the circumstances of this offender and the offense? The formal process of the courts allows for various opinions to be expressed on the matter before the judge decides. The offender speaks, then the victim and the prosecutor. Sometimes family members of the victim and the offender are also encouraged to offer an opinion; and occasionally experts, such as psychiatrists, give testimony. Whatever penalty is eventually selected, however, must conform to the requirements of the law, and some choices are not allowed in a given penal code. Certain crimes are so serious that at a minimum, a sentence to prison is required; other crimes are sufficiently mundane that financial or community penalties can be imposed.

In the last thirty years, many reformers have become concerned about disparities in penal sanctions (Allen 1996) and have tried to develop penal codes that resulted in more consistency in sentencing. These new sentencing approaches, whether sentencing guidelines or determinate sentencing (Tonry 1993), have been seen by some as successful and by others as a mistake. But they all have had the result of reducing the range of penalties a judge may consider when imposing sentence. In most jurisdictions across America, judges today have far fewer choices available to them when determining the sentence than they did a generation ago, because legal reforms have restricted those choices.

Community justice challenges the sanctioning function of the courts in two ways. First, those who advocate for community-oriented penalties tend to desire a broader array of possible case outcomes than are now available to judges. They approve of creative sanctioning that builds a penalty based partly on the crime, but also very much on the circumstances of the offender. They also call for a sentence that takes into account the desire of the community for a long-term investment in public safety. Community justice advocates also give a very high priority to what is thought of as "voice": the victim, the offender, and the community ought to have an opportunity to explore and explain what is desired as the best outcome of the sanction, once it is selected. Perhaps the biggest way community justice challenges the sanctioning function of the courts is that, under its model, sentences are not "imposed" by a judge who is remote to the circumstances of the case; rather, the penalty is determined in interaction with those who were affected by the crime, including the offender.

How courts work today

We have a view of the courts as a very formal, dignified process. Judges sit high above the courtroom, donned in severe black robes. Lawyers, dressed with professional respect, speak only when allowed. Decorum is at a premium. A kind of ritual occurs, starting with the "Oyez, oyez," and punctuated by the ringing authority of the judge's gavel. The courtroom is purposefully designed to symbolize the somber majesty of the law, standing in for the historical prerogative of the omnipotent Crown. Each detail of the way the court is arranged speaks of the power and dignity of the law, and the comparative insignificance of those who are assembled under its austerity.

Is that the way the law really operates in practice?

The contemporary courtroom maintains elements of this stylish, symbolic instrument of power and authority. But for the vast majority of cases, what happens bears only a minuscule resemblance to this picture. To understand the way the criminal trial courts work today, we must begin with four concepts: caseload pressure, informality, exchange, and stages of decision making.

Caseload pressure is a dominant force in contemporary courts because the number of criminal cases to be processed by the courts has grown over the last 30 years without a commensurate increase in the number of judges, prosecutors, and defenders. State courts experienced a 45 percent increase in criminal filings between 1984 and 1997 (Ostrom and Kauder 1998). Court players have felt this growth. State prosecutors reported that the volume of their caseloads has increased because more offenders are being prosecuted (Nugent and McEwan 1988); and public defenders, who receive on average 80 percent of all criminal cases, have not had increases in staff commensurate with increases in caseloads (Spangenber Group 2001). Specifically, this means that there is a premium on avoiding jury trials, which are five to 10 times more costly in time and personnel than guilty pleas or even (in many cases) bench trials. Even though defendants have a constitutional right to select a jury trial, the realities of case pressure mean that lawyers on all sides will try to resolve a case without resorting to an expensive and in many cases, unnecessary, jury trial.

Jury trials are not necessary in many cases because the factual guilt of the defendant is often not in question. Of course, the state must be able to prove the defendant's guilt in a trial, but often there is incontrovertible evidence of guilt, and the prospects of acquittal are less than slim. In such cases, what defendants have at stake is less a question of adjudication than the eventual sanction to be imposed. Here, *informality* is in the interests of all parties. Rather than simply leave the sanction up to the judge, it is often thought better for the state and the defendant to reach a general agreement about a sanction acceptable to both parties. To do this requires informal conversation and negotiation outside the inflexible confines of the courtroom.

Flexibility is reinforced by the reality of *exchange,* which means that each party has something to offer the other in the process of negotiating a case outcome. The defender can promise not to demand an expensive jury trial and can promise the unparalleled efficiency of a guilty plea instead of a trial. The prosecutor can offer an opportunity to avoid some of the harsher penalties available under the law, either through reducing the charges or agreeing to make a recommendation to the court for a lenient sentence. The judge, by accepting this negotiated settlement, can avoid tying up the courtroom with an unneeded criminal trial in which guilt is not at issue, and can thereby avoid delaying the getting to more pressing cases.

The *stages of decision making* in the courts facilitate this less formal processing of cases. In most courts, there is an initial hearing in which the charges are registered and the basic evidence on behalf of those charges is listed. Often an arraignment follows, with a more formal reading of charges and evidence, a formal plea by the defendant, and a date set for a trial. There are pretrial hearing dates that deal with questions such as bail and the admissibility of evidence. All this occurs prior to the actual trial, and each event offers an opportunity for the parties to discuss, informally and outside the presence of the judge, a way of resolving the charges without going to trial. Each stage accelerates the pressure on the parties to work out a nonjury decision, and each stage offers a new opportunity to discuss a way to make a nonjury agreement work.

The combination of caseload pressure, exchange, and a tradition of informality dominates the stages of the court process. Because there are repeated opportunities to reach an agreement, a trial is usually avoided in favor of a negotiated guilty plea. This means that most defendants eventually waive their constitutional rights to a trial, to proof of the charges "beyond a reasonable doubt," to avoid self-incrimination, and to have all the prosecution's evidence tested against rules of admissibility. The defendant trades these constitutional rights in expectation of a penalty that is less onerous than the one threatened by full force of the law.

It is against this backdrop that the contemporary community justice movement in the courts must be evaluated. Critics of the community justice model argue that a defendant's rights are imperiled by the informality of decision making in community-oriented courts, and the basic protections of the law are lost. They also say that negotiated decision making results in compromises that detract from the symbolic importance of the formal criminal law. There is also a concern that too much discretion will lead to sanctions in a community justice framework that suffer from extensive sentencing disparity.

In fact, the current system encourages these same problems because its procedures in full expression are so expensive, and because those who are involved in the system have very good reasons for avoiding the most extreme implications of the provisions of the penal law. The question is not whether community justice has too much informality and negotiation of its practices but whether the informality and negotiation activity within community justice practices leads to case outcomes that are more acceptable to all parties.

The victim of crime

The last two decades have seen increasing importance placed on the victims of crime. This concern has expressed itself in two forms. First, there has been strong pressure to increase the severity of sanctions in the belief that tougher penalties show respect for the impact of crime on victims. Second, there has been pressure on the formal criminal justice system to listen more to victims regarding the way cases are handled. Thus, prosecutors have opened up victim-assistance offices, and penal-code reforms have created a basis for victims to speak at sentencing and parole hearings, and even to be informed of the way charges are changed during plea negotiations.

The addition of the voice of the victim has changed the dynamics of the criminal court case-management practices. Victims are given a very limited role when they are encouraged to testify at trial and allowed to make a sentencing recommendation. But a more aggressive stance regarding victims lets them have a say about the case at every stage. It includes them as a voice in the charging process, the negotiations of a guilty plea, and the selection of the eventual penal sanction. Nowhere are victims as fully involved in the criminal justice process as they could be, but every criminal court hears much more from victims today than was the case 20 years ago.

Now that we have become more understanding of the needs of victims and more willing to give them a substantial voice in the criminal justice process, we have become more sophisticated in our appreciation of what victims need in order to begin to recover from the emotional and material costs of the crime. It is not always what we might think. Studies of victims find that they differ in their needs (Office for Victims of Crime 2000). Some want a kind of revenge, while others are more interested in restitution. Some want to meet and confront the offender; others do not. Some want to understand why the crime happened, and these victims often look for a way for the offender to be rehabilitated so that future criminality will not occur. Others care little about what is in the offender's head or heart. They just want a meaningful punishment to be imposed by the court.

Almost all victims want to be able to speak on their own behalf, and being able to give voice to their experiences in the formal justice process is often an important part of recovery from crime. By far, most victims, when given a choice, would prefer a sanction that leads the offender to a productive, law-abiding life, over a sanction that merely punishes. But almost all victims think that some form of punishment is called for in order to bring the case to closure. Contemporary critics of the way the court system handles victims point out that there is little capacity for the justice system to undertake the variety of strategies required to meet the diverse concerns of crime victims, and there is almost no provision for handling cases differently based on the desires of the victim.

We know as well that the reality of the victim's circumstances does not always correspond to the popular image of the victim. We often think emotionally about the victim of crime, and in our image we see an entirely innocent stranger, victimized by a cavalier felon. However, most victims are not strangers to their victimizer – many are family members, and others are acquaintances. In these cases, there is often an understandable ambivalence about harsh punishment for the perpetrator of the offense. Just as important, crimes such as drug abuse or prostitution have no obvious victim. How to represent the voice of the victim in these quite common circumstances is an essential part of a broad victims movement in criminal justice.

A growing number of federal and state prosecutors' offices now employ victim advocates that can assist the victim in understanding and navigating the criminal justice system. Victim advocates are helpful for not only the primary victims, the one against whom the offense occurred, but also secondary victims, close relatives of the primary victims. Victim advocates work closely with social workers and mental health professionals to provide support for those victims who are suffering. While emotional support of the victim is important, victim advocates may do their best work in talking with the victims about the technical aspects of the court processes. It can be very disconcerting for a victim attending a preliminary hearing to find out that the judge has decided to suppress a piece of evidence without knowing what that process entails or how it will affect their case. Victim advocates can explain the actions of the judge and the prosecutors so victims will have a better understanding of the processes and arcane language that is being used.

In some jurisdictions prosecutors are consulting with victims about prosecution issues and seeking their input prior to filing charges. While this does not mean that the professional prosecutor is putting the decision to prosecute in the hands of the victims, it does insure that the prosecutor will have the support of the victim should his or her testimony be required. Recently, in a case involving the prosecution of a serial murderer in Jackson County, Missouri, the prosecutor called together all of the victims' families to discuss prosecution strategies. The suspect had committed 12 murders over an extended period of time and, as often the case, evidence was stronger in some crimes than it was in others, especially since many of the victims led a high-risk lifestyle. The prosecutor wanted the families to understand why he had chosen to file charges in just a few of the cases so the families would not feel as though their loved one was less important than those victims whose cases would be filed. After the private meeting with the families the prosecutor conducted a news conference to announce which cases would be prosecuted and why the decision had been made. Attending the news conference were the families of the majority of the victims and after the news conference they affirmed their support for the decision and the prosecutor. Prosecutorial actions such as this strengthen the trust between the community and the prosecutor by providing respect for the losses suffered by the victims' families. This was especially important in this situation since the primary victims were not wealthy or influential persons but instead victims who are often seen by society as less worthy of receiving justice.

The increasing role of the crime victim in the justice system is a critical development in the advent of community justice, because those who believe in community justice have had to invent new ways to incorporate victim sentiments and interests into the community justice ethic. From the community justice standpoint, of course, the broader community suffers from crime, so delivering justice in the community helps deal with the problem of victims insofar as they are community members. Moreover, the process of sanctioning offenders affects their families and their communities, and the community justice approach makes room for these issues. There is, however, a need for more – a need for community justice to embrace the specific concerns of specific victims of crime.

The community court

The idea of community-oriented strategies in the courts has become a new and very important force in recent years. Today, community courts are a popular idea, with many urban areas experimenting with community-based specialty courts. As we shall see, the community court concept applies to courts that serve particular neighborhoods within larger jurisdictions, and it also refers to courts that deal with a particular community of clients, such as domestic-violence cases. But the contemporary idea of community courts borrows some concepts from an era long past in the court system when municipal courts held extraordinary power over adjudication in communities that were isolated from other governmental sectors. The environment for community courts has changed a great deal in modern times, but some of the values we expect of them have not.

A historical look at community courts

During most of US history, trial courts have been community based. Until the early part of the twentieth century, American society was a rural society in which county legal government was the dominant political force. Counties had a criminal court, located in the county seat, and justice emanated from that venue. The benefit of these courts was their fit to the community. The judges who determined criminal cases lived in their communities, knew many of the residents, and had a sense of the values that the community held. Their activity was far from impersonal and held strongly to themes of community values.

This was also the main weakness of the community-friendly rural court. People who were community outcasts or whose status in the community was suspect may have found it hard to receive equal justice. This charge held particularly in the South, where Blacks encountered an often-hostile court system run exclusively by the dominant White majority. The all-too-common lack of sympathy for poor Blacks in trouble with the law exposed the dark underbelly of community-friendly courts: if you were not seen as a legitimate part of the community, you might have had a little trouble getting justice.

This concern fueled a professional version of the courts that became the dominant idea in the latter half of the twentieth century. Several key issues featured in this change; chief among them was that the work of the courts was not community work but was a professional task requiring technical skills. The law, it was felt, needed to be uniform across all places, and a community-friendly judiciary was inconsistent with the vision of an unvarying criminal law. Part of this sentiment came from an evolving commitment to equal protection under the law, which arose as part of an emerging concern for civil rights and rights of the powerless. Another concern came from the sense that "amateur" justice was inadequate, often stemming from a faulty understanding of the law and a parochial application of its principles. There was also, in the last third of the century, a new concern for equality in punishments. Punishment disparity was identified as a serious problem in criminal law, and the remedy was thought to be the reduction of sentencing discretion in favor of application of a set of sentencing standards in every location of the jurisdiction.

The romantic vision of a community-friendly court, as existed in the early rural and agrarian United States, is forever gone, replaced by professional civil servants highly trained in the legal process. Yet the community court is not extinct. Most Americans may live in urban and suburban settings, where a sense of personal anonymity is a common part of legal procedures. But most of the jurisdictions in the United States remain small and medium-sized, and many of America's courts serve populations that are not the urban, disenfranchised poor. The state of Indiana, for example, has 92 counties, and each has a county seat with a county court that handles criminal cases arising in that jurisdiction. Of those 92 courthouses, perhaps a dozen serve populations that can be considered primarily densely urban.

However, the contemporary community court movement is not designed for the rural or even the suburban courthouse. The way people describe the mission of the community court places its relevance directly within the troubled neighborhoods in our densely populated urban areas. The neighborhoods served are discrete locations existing wholly within larger, more heterogeneous jurisdictions. The communities served within those neighborhoods are typically poor groups lacking access to legal resources. What has happened is that the logic of the bygone community court, which can tailor its efforts to better meet the needs of the community it serves, has been reformulated as an urban solution to distinctly urban problems.

Thus, we can make a distinction between community-friendly courts that operate in smaller community settings and are composed of community leaders who handle cases involving people who, for the most part, know each other, and the modern community-oriented court. This latter version is not a happenstance of the nature of a community, but is an intentional innovation designed to help create a sense of community and improve the feel of the community it serves.

The contemporary community court movement

The breakthrough example was the Midtown Community Court in New York City. Developed in 1993, the Midtown Community Court was the brainchild of the Midtown Business Improvement District (BID) coalition of businesses, prominent residents, and social services operating in the Times Square area of New York City. The Times Square area has a concentration of entertainment-based businesses – theaters, restaurants, hotels, and recreational game centers – and therefore attracted a large number of one-day "tourists." By the late 1980s, misbehavior by some of the more disagreeable visitors had become a serious concern: drunken and disorderly, the "tourists" would urinate in the streets and alleys, openly solicit prostitutes, get in fights with each other, and engage in other loud and rowdy activity. The increasingly undesirable nature of these visitors made living in the residential areas surrounding the businesses an ever more distressing experience.

One of the problems was that the criminal justice system was largely unresponsive to the situation. Arrests would be made, and perpetrators would spend the night in a holding cell nearby. Then they would be released, only to return to Midtown and engage in the same disruptive behavior. The sentences imposed were typically for "time served," and referrals to treatment were never given, so the problem people and their problem behaviors remained. And in a classic broken windows pattern, their presence in the area attracted others like them.

Led by criminal justice innovator Gretchen Dykstra, who was the CEO of the BID, a new strategy was invented. People arrested in the Times Square area would not be taken elsewhere to be processed by courts having no accountability to the Midtown community. Instead, they would be booked, arraigned, and adjudicated by the local Midtown Community Court, newly established solely to serve cases arising from this area of Manhattan. Not only would these cases be handled locally, but they would also be sanctioned locally. Sanctions would include requirements of public service – a typical offender sentenced by the court does community service cleaning the Midtown streets – but the offenders would also be placed in court-administered treatment programs. The latter, involving substance-abuse treatment, job-training assistance, job-placement assistance, anger-management treatment, and so forth, set the Midtown Community Court apart from the other courts in New York City. Whereas those courts focused their attention on serious felonies that made citizens fearful of their streets and often did next to nothing about nuisance crimes, the Midtown Court reasoned that it was precisely these public order offenses that led to deterioration in the Midtown area.

Residents and businesses banded together to form the Midtown Community Court, and they were wildly enthusiastic about its accomplishments. The popularity of that experimental court with its core clients – the businesses and residents of Midtown – was matched by the appreciation many of the court's criminal clients expressed for the services they received. Soon, the experiment was seen as such a complete success that community courts began to spring up in other urban locations. The Center for Court Innovation, which designed and ran the Midtown Community Court, began to assist other locations in developing their own community courts for problem locations. In 1999, the National Institute of Justice funded a series of community courts across the nation on an experimental basis.

The Midtown Community Court is not without its critics, some of whom argue that locating social services within the courthouse merely serves to strengthen judicial institutions at the expense of the community institutions the court was ostensibly created to help. This criticism is more meaningful in light of the unavoidable added expense of establishing a community court. There are ancillary costs associated with decentralizing court services, such as the extra personnel costs for defense, prosecution, and corrections. Some critics have claimed, in fact, that only in business-rich Midtown Manhattan can a community court garner sufficient resources to be able to create a true problem-solving court, one that disposes of cases on a local level and is actually able to provide the care needed to address the complex problems faced by low-level offenders. Consequently, the community court model is not truly replicable. Community courts, most of which target low-level offenders, are also subject to the charge that they engage in "net-widening" activity. By bringing into the criminal justice arena a whole class of offenders who otherwise would have little if no contact with the justice system, community courts may be serving to criminalize and punish individuals who might be better served with more informal, community-based censure for their behavior. Moreover, by displacing normal venues for informal, community-based censure, community courts actually serve to debilitate the inherent social institutions that are the foundation of public safety in neighborhoods. But even with the validity of these concerns, the community court movement has become a bellwether for reformulating courts to make them more accountable to the communities they serve.

Box 3.1 Center for Court Innovation

The Center for Court Innovation (CCI), established as a public–private partnership, serves as the research and development arm of the New York State Unified Court System. CCI pioneered the first community court in Midtown Manhattan in 1993 and has since been in the forefront of the movement to develop and promote community and problem-solving courts. Building on their success with the Midtown model, CCI tested the flexibility of its community court approach in two disparate neighborhoods: Red Hook, Brooklyn, and Harlem, New York. In each of these sites, CCI worked to be responsive to local concerns. The Red Hook Community Justice Center, which houses the nation's first multijurisdictional court, also incorporates an adult job-training program and a youth court. Harlem residents were primarily concerned about the impact of youth crime on the neighborhood. Consequently, in addition to being a housing and re-entry court, the Harlem Community Justice Center is home to a youth court, a youth mediation program, and a juvenile treatment court. Thus, by incorporating outreach to the community during the planning process, CCI ensured that the courts were truly responsive to community public safety issues and had laid the groundwork for ongoing community involvement.

Community-oriented court functions

The two main functions of the courts are adjudication and sanctioning, and each has been open to an infusion of community justice concepts. We will explore how community justice principles have been incorporated into traditional court functions.

Community-oriented adjudication

Adjudication consists of three roles: prosecution, defense, and judiciary. Each can be adapted to a community context, though the most experience exists with community-oriented prosecution. Because the three roles are so tightly linked, it makes sense to consider the ways that creating one as a community-based model leads to the logic of the other.

Community prosecution

Michael Shrunk of Multnomah County (Portland), Oregon, had been elected as district attorney and served for nine years, and most people thought of him as having a "safe" seat. He enjoyed the wide respect of the electorate, the confidence of business leaders, and political independence. Yet he had a problem. In the highest crime area of Portland, the Lloyd District, people had little confidence in the criminal justice system, and his prosecutors often faced difficulty obtaining citizen support for investigations and prosecutions of everyday offenders from that area.

Shrunk decided to try something new. He opened up a district attorney branch office in the neighborhood and assigned one of his more talented assistant district attorneys (ADA) to that office. While most of his "downtown" ADAs were specialists in particular types of offenses – frauds, homicide, drugs – this ADA would handle all the cases emanating from that neighborhood. It was an experiment to see how this energetic ADA could change the relationship between the prosecutor's office and the residents of that area of Portland.

The innovation worked. After a few months, the ADA had gained the confidence of many of the residents of the area, and new, productive relationships were formed between the citizenry and the prosecution. No longer did the residents of that area have an alienated, or even hostile, relationship to the work of the prosecutor. The residents wanted legal help with their community problems, especially problems that related to public safety and community quality of life, and the new community prosecutor could help them with that.

Just as interesting was the way the prosecutor's job changed when the office was moved to the problem neighborhood. In the downtown office, the emphasis was on major cases, the kinds that make headlines and involve severe violence to victims: rape, murder, and assault. It was natural for the downtown prosecutors to focus on these cases because they seemed to be the most important. The public also considered these cases important, but there was an even more avid interest in the kinds of criminal activity that were less likely to make headlines in the local newspaper. Citizens wanted crack houses to be closed down, street drug markets to be moved off public space, open prostitution to be removed from their streets, and landlord violations to be prosecuted. They also wanted their kids who were in trouble with the law to get help, by being placed in treatment programs and getting assistance with education and employment.

What the community ADA learned was that serious crime may be a high priority to outsiders, but the people who live in those problems places may have a different priority. Most people think that people in high-crime areas want tough prosecution of serious criminal cases, but this idea misses the myriad, everyday indignities that people in these places must confront. What they want is something like a legal service; they need access to the courts to press for solutions to their community-level problems. They have asked for help in problem solving in addition to the prosecution of individual criminal cases. They want a legally relevant support system for their community priorities, and the prosecutor, as an official of the court, has a unique ability to provide that service. Because this kind of law is so different, some people have referred to it as "community safety law" (Conner and Griffin 1998).

The Portland lesson has been repeated in numerous other jurisdictions where community prosecutors have begun to reshape the prosecution function in multi-problem neighborhoods. The problems vary from location to location because in each community, there is a slightly different set of issues to be tackled. But the big picture is the same everywhere. Whenever a centralized prosecution service has opened up specialized offices to serve a particular, troubled location, there has been an increase in citizen confidence in the prosecutor's activity, and there has been a shift in that activity to better match the needs and desires of the citizenry who live there.

However, there have been problems with community prosecution. Community-based prosecutors are open to co-optation by community groups by developing too close or comfortable a relationship with a select number of citizens. This co-optation jeopardizes their neutrality and inhibits their ability to see the full range of problems that need to be addressed in a neighborhood. Community prosecutors must also be careful about burnout. In the face of the multiple and varied problems that communities face, prosecutors may try to take on too much. But it must be recognized that community prosecution has emerged as a new way to provide prosecutorial services so that communities' needs for legal assistance with public safety problems can be addressed.

Gray (2008) says that the growth of community prosecution since the 1990s has been significant and that community-based approaches to practicing law can now be found in law school curriculum. Unfortunately, there has still been little empirical data collected on the effectiveness of community prosecution in preventing and reducing crime. Gray recognizes the difficulty in evaluating this method of prosecution through the examination of the prevention of crime, but she notes that the American Prosecutors Research Institute (APRI) and the Bureau of Justice Assistance (BJA) have both developed systems that prosecutors can use to measure the effectiveness of community prosecution techniques.

Gray explains that APRI suggests attention to establishing long-term and intermediate goals through community needs assessments. According to APRI, performance measures should include not only the traditional methods of measurement but also decreasing the fear of crime by residents, improving overall quality of life, and ensuring justice for victims of crime. APRI provides consulting and guides to assist prosecutors in implementing community prosecution methods. BJA recommends an evaluation model that divides impact measures into implementation and impact sections. The implementation section allows prosecutors to review progress in the area of community prosecution and determine the maturity of the program. After completion of this needs assessment, future planning can be conducted before moving into the outcome measure phase. Evaluation in the impact section would focus on achieving the goals that were established during the planning phase and would include measuring impact in the areas of target problem, target area, role of the community, content of community prosecution strategy, and technical elements of the prosecutor's office such as office organization and workload. One concern cited by Gray is the lack of established and accepted guidelines to assists prosecutors in establishing community prosecution. She also notes that guidelines provided by APRI and BJA are very helpful and they point out the fact that there is no one right size or method for establishing this type of a program. Finally, Gray notes that community prosecution still allows for proper prosecutorial discretion but with that discretion come new issues about ethical concerns that should be addressed.

Community defender services

Much newer than the idea of community prosecution is the development of community defenders, also called neighborhood defender services. As a result, there are very few studies of this application of the community justice idea in the court area.

Neighborhood defenders would seem to have several advantages over the traditional, downtown and centralized defender services. For example, the neighborhood defender is closer to the community where the defendant lives, and it is often easier to obtain witnesses in support of the defendant at trial and to speak on behalf of the defendant at sentencing. Because many of the crimes occur in the same neighborhood where the defendant lives, it is also easier to gather evidence in those cases that result in a trial.

An equally important advantage of neighborhood-based defender services is that the defender gets to know the neighborhood. Relationships are established with important private-sector interests – such as businesses and churches – and these can translate into valuable supports for clients. Businesses can jobs for clients, and churches can provide other types of assistance. Familiarity with social-service providers can also establish a foundation for clients to deal with the problems that led to their criminal involvement.

This point highlights one of the key differences between neighborhood-based defender services and traditional services. In the latter, the lawyer sees the job as getting the best deal possible for the client – a finding of not guilty, if possible, and a short sentence, if necessary. But the neighborhood defender looks at the broader interests of the defendant, helping the defendant get into drug treatment, for example, or arranging child care and family services for the family members who are not under scrutiny of the court.

As happens for neighborhood-based prosecutors, defenders who work at the neighborhood level find that their job changes. They are no longer exclusively concerned with the tactics of the criminal case. Instead, they also develop an interest in the defendant's relationships to the neighborhood, and they look for ways to strengthen the client's integration into the neighborhood.

Box 3.2 Neighborhood Defender Service

Launched in 1990 by the Vera Institute of Justice, the Neighborhood Defender Service (NDS) in Harlem, New York, completely altered the traditional nature of indigent legal representation. Based in the community, NDS does not wait for the court to assign it cases; rather, through community outreach it encourages residents to call when they are first arrested – much the way wealthy clients call their attorneys. This gives NDS more time to develop cases and potentially resolve them before they go to court. Using a team approach that includes an attorney, community worker, administrative assist-ant, intern, and senior attorney, NDS shifts the priority of legal representation from cases that are in trial to the up-front work that occurs when defendants first walk in the door. As a result, teams handle far more than the case at hand and help to mediate and dispose of community problems that are often shunted through the court system for lack of a community-based response. NDS finds that their clients lead complicated lives; many do not perceive their criminal case as a priority among the many others they face. By listening to their clients, NDS adopts a more holistic approach to legal representation, which often takes a backseat to addressing other concerns, such as implications of the case for the family. NDS also works proactively to improve public safety in the community. Recognizing a need in the community for legal education, NDS leads workshops with young people, teaching them how to prevent potential conflict with police from escalating.

Community judiciary

We have discussed the concept of the community court, and the head of that court, the judge, might represent a type of community judiciary. As yet, however, there is no official role for a community judiciary beyond what we described for com-munity courts. However, as community courts gain acceptance, there is reason to think that a kind of community-oriented judiciary will also grow.

Such a judiciary would be very different from the centralized, disconnected judges of today. They would work closely with citizen groups and neighborhood interests to develop a judicial practice in behalf of neighborhood concerns. This role would con-stantly test their commitment to judicial impartiality, but it would also open a door to a deeper and more effective level of citizen participation in the work of the courts.

In effect, the judiciary can follow the orientation of the defender and prosecutor. If they have devoted themselves to a community justice model, the way they develop their cases and the way they hope to resolve disputes will be oriented to the community. The judicial role will then be presented with case decisions and caseload priorities that reflect the orientation of the attorneys.

Community-oriented sanctioning

It is one thing to identify and prioritize criminal complaints with an eye to community issues; it is quite another to try to resolve them with that same vision. Community justice sanctioning offers a significant departure from the usual strategy, because both the aims of the sanction and the stakeholders to the outcome are different.

Under traditional models of sanctioning, the aims of the criminal sentence are primarily punitive, especially for serious crime. The sentence may include recognition of the possibility of rehabilitation, if an offender is required to attend a treatment program or placed under some form of community supervision with treatment conditions. But the overarching value expressed by the sentence is punitive, as its centerpiece is a loss of freedom. Secondary aims of traditional criminal sentences may be incapacitation or deterrence, depending upon the circumstances of the case. The main point is that the object of the sentence is to do something *to* the offender that will communicate blame and reprobation through a penalty that is intentionally unpleasant. (For a discussion of this idea, see C. S. Lewis, *The Abolition of Man*.)

In this model, the sentence is determined with little attention paid to anyone but the offender. There may be sympathy expressed to the victim and an emotional appeal to community values, but the sentence is about the offender's conduct and the requirements of the law. In a very real sense, the crime is seen as a trespass against the laws of the state, and the resolution of the crime is for the state to reassert its authority by imposing a penalty for the trespass.

Community justice changes the aims of the sentence. Punishment of the wrongdoer is not eliminated as a goal, but it takes a second priority to the needs of the community for an outcome that restores some of the losses suffered as a result of the crime. Instead of viewing the crime as a legal dispute between the accused and the state, a criminal act is seen as an unfair loss (or harm) imposed by one citizen upon another. The problem to be solved is to overcome the unfairness by restoring the loss and repairing the harm. In most crimes, there are multiple victims – a citizen, the community, relatives of the offender and the victim – and finding a way to restore all their losses is a priority. In this way, the stakeholders to a criminal event are not just the state and the accused, but everyone affected by the crime.

Thomson (2009) argues that much of the use by the courtroom workgroup of the penalty-oriented model is due to mundane decisions where the group exercises actions that are comfortable and familiar. He boldly suggests that a large amount of sentencing is guesswork because of the lack of information considered by the court in pronouncing sentences and that, together with considerations of liberty and equality, should lead us to err on the side of avoiding incarceration whenever possible. Thomson cites the growing body of research over the past 25 years that indicates public opinion supports moderation in criminal sentencing. He believes that a model of progressive justice that emphasizes moderation in punishment pursued in conjunction with a restorative justice perspective would provide community well-being sentencing with solid grounding in traditional jurisprudence. The ultimate goal for Thomson would be to lower the number of offenders sentenced to incarceration and allow community input into the proper sentencing that would strengthen the community and rehabilitate the offender.

The role of victims

In this philosophy of sanctioning, the role of the victim is radically changed. Traditional justice models tend to see the victim as aligned with the punitive agenda of the state. They stand mostly at the sidelines of the criminal case, offering testimony in support of the conviction and being given the opportunity to argue for the most punitive sanction available to the court. To the extent there has been harm or loss as a result of the crime, it tends to be expressed as anger at the offender and a call for a more punitive penalty.

Studies of victims find that many have a much more complex view of how they would like the sanctioning process to proceed and what they expect from the penalty (Office for Victims of Crime 2000). Most want the offender to be punished for the crime, but they also want to be able to tell their story so the offender can see how the criminal act was harmful. They want to understand why the offender committed the crime and to see a sanction that makes it less likely that the offender will repeat the crime. If some sort of rehabilitation program is in order, the victim usually supports its inclusion in the sanction; and victims want some support that will help to repair the harm they have encountered as a result of the crime.

Box 3.3 Parallel justice

The movement toward incorporating victims' voices in the justice process is best represented by Susan Herman, the executive director of the National Center for Victims of Crime, who has called for a system of parallel justice for victims. She argues that most victims don't get a chance to participate in the justice process because their offenders were never arrested or prosecuted, and even those that do participate are likely to be disappointed because the justice system is focused primarily on instituting appropriate treatment of offenders. Rather than tie the dispensation of victims' services to the court process and offender restitution, local government authorities should provide all victims with resources ranging from counseling to new door locks to victims' compensation. Herman sees the creation of this parallel system for victims taking place on the local level. Local leaders would be "challenged to assess the needs of victims in their community, establish a process for meeting those needs, and combine federal and local resources to make parallel justice a reality" (Herman 2000).

These views are similar to those of citizens at large (Gorczyk and Perry 1997). Most people want a penalty that "makes sense," in that it will help to restore the victim. They also want the offender to recognize the harmfulness of the act and regret it. This desire translates into an "instrumental penance," where the offender is so sorry for the act that he or she takes strong steps to deal with the problems that led to the act so it will not be repeated. In this sense, the community expects an offender to repent, make restitution to the victim and the community, and become a better citizen. The desire is for a three-way restoration – of the victim, the community, and the offender.

To achieve this three-way restoration, community justice has to place the victim and the community in the center of the sanctioning process, not at the sideline. Instead of a process that emphasizes the voice of the prosecution and the protests of the offender, community justice seeks a process that gives voice to victims, offenders, and communities, and moves the role of the judge and prosecutor to the sideline. This approach is known as "restorative justice."

Restorative justice

Restorative justice is a new version of an ancient idea: the outcome of a transgression against the community ought to be some process that restores the community from the effects of that transgression and thereby allows the transgressor to be restored as well. There are four main versions of restorative justice (Bazemore and Umbreit, 2001).

Victim–offender mediation is an approach to sanctioning that enables the victim to confront the offender with the harm that has been done, and then invokes a process whereby the victim and offender come to an agreement about the appropriate sanction to be imposed as a consequence of the wrongful conduct.

Community reparative boards are citizen tribunals that receive criminally convicted referrals from the court, for which they determine the appropriate sanctions through a process of conversation with the offender and others affected by the crime.

Family group conferencing is derived from ancient practices of the Maori people of New Zealand, in which the family of the offender, the victim, and the community come together with a trained facilitator to develop an appropriate sanction for the offender's misconduct.

Circle sentencing is based upon traditional practices of aboriginal peoples of North America, in which community leaders, the offender, and the victim come together in a circle to seek sanctions that will lead to healing from the crime on everyone's part.

There is a growing body of research on restorative justice approaches. These studies find that most restorative justice processes are limited to nonviolent, less serious crime, although there are a handful of projects that apply these principles to interpersonal violent crime. Almost all studies report a significant improvement in the satisfaction of both victims and offenders with the process and the sanction it produced. Several studies show that offenders who go through restorative sanctions have lower failure rates than those who go through the traditional process, though other studies find no difference. Interestingly, there is some evidence emerging that the most successful restorative justice projects are those that allow cases involving serious interpersonal violence and that are not restricted to property crime (Coates and Umbreit 1999).

Methods of Alternative Dispute Resolution (ADR) have assisted in the growth of reconciliation programs. Three elements of ADR are conciliation, mediation, and arbitration. Conciliation involves using a contact person to facilitate information flow from one disputant to another. Mediation, which was also discussed in Chapter 2, involves negotiation between disputants with an independent third party helping the parties to arrive at a mutually acceptable compromise. The process involves discussion, sharing of viewpoints, and the discovery of areas of common interest. Arbitration involves the use of a neutral individual who hears both sides of the dispute and then imposes a decision based upon the information gathered during the investigation.

Karmen (2010) argues that the growing interest in informal justice is furthered by several beliefs. First is the belief that centralized government coercion has not brought about social change. Second, the belief that non-stranger conflicts should be settled in arenas outside of the formal court system. The final belief is that the formal punishment and rehabilitation effort behind bars has failed to "cure" offenders. With courts and prisons facing capacity, informal alternatives to dispute resolution is appealing according to Karmen.

Karmen also recognizes that there could be problems with the increased use of restorative justice techniques. If caseloads grow too large there could be a temptation to adopt procedures that hurry cases through the process, causing less than thorough treatment of the disputes brought for resolution. Another concern is that restorative justice programs remain victim-centered with an emphasis on offender responsibility for the offense committed. Finally, restorative justice cannot be sold as a cure-all that will be applicable to all criminal matters. The use of restorative justice has been successful in many juvenile cases and in property-oriented crime. Increased use of the techniques in interpersonal crime should explored, but it must be recognized that not all interpersonal crime is amenable to this resolution technique. All in all, restorative justice appears to be a viable tool for a justice system that prides itself on the proper administration of justice while allowing sentencing that strengthens the fabric of the community.

Courts for specialized communities

As new adjudication practices emerged and sanctioning schemes broadened, more attention came to be paid to the way the courts were structured to accommodate these processes. When increasing specialization of treatment and intervention protocols that address the needs and circumstances of specific populations, such as substance abusers or juvenile delinquents, were added to the mix, courts began to tailor their work to these special communities of offenders.

Drug courts

Drug courts emerged in response to the crack epidemic of the late 1980s, which flooded court dockets with drug offenders. The initial drug-court models were established to overcome the backlog of cases through expedited case processing. These courts, however, did not address the "revolving-door" phenomenon of the many addicted offenders who inevitably became recidivists upon release. Drug courts as commonly implemented today coordinate legal case processing with a range of treatment modalities. These courts build on the experience of pioneers such as Treatment Alternatives to Street Crime (TASC), which brought a link of treatment into the courtroom, but take this treatment intervention one step further through a codified model of "therapeutic jurisprudence." There are now more than 600 drug courts in operation across the country, a number that includes juvenile treatment courts and family treatment courts, as well as drug courts (see Federal Department of Justice, Office of Justice Programs, Drug Court Clearinghouse and Technical Assistance Project at http://www.ncjrs.org /drug_courts /training.html#2).

In a drug court, the judge plays an active role in helping defendants conquer their addiction by teaching consequential thinking through a series of graduated sanctions and rewards. Defendants are required to appear in front of the judge at frequent and regular intervals, at which point they recount how they are progressing with their treatment and other life goals. Compliance with the court requirements is celebrated by rewards, such as having to appear in court less frequently, and non-compliance is marked by sanctions that vary in severity depending on the gravity of the violation. Low-level rearrest might trigger a temporary remand to jail, while a urine test positive for drugs will bring a day spent in court watching the proceedings. These graduated sanctions incorporate an understanding that relapse is an almost unavoidable component of the recovery process, and rather than terminate someone from treatment for relapse, the court incorporates an appropriate therapeutic response. Defendants who successfully complete the drug court often receive a reduced sentence, a lowered or dismissed charge, or some combination.

As in most community justice models, the justice player roles are redefined. In order to operate a drug court effectively, the traditionally adversarial roles of the prosecutor, defense, and judge are shifted so that the three represent a coordinated team. This team then acts both to safeguard public safety and to treat defendants for their addiction problems. Drug courts also serve as community justice models, not because they are located within a geographic community and therefore concern themselves with the problems of that community, but because their approach to justice problems incorporates a context much larger than the case at hand. Drug courts work to solve the problem of drug-addicted offenders who cycle in and out of the justice system. To do this, the court must form strong links to community-based treatment programs by bringing them into the courtroom and the justice process. Additionally, drug courts often develop connections to other community-based support services such as job training and education. In the ideal drug-court model, community volunteers would be brought into the court to provide continual support for defendants in court and upon their return to the community.

Domestic violence courts

Domestic violence continues to be one of the most intractable public safety issues with which communities and the justice system grapple daily. The National Crime Victimization Survey revealed that in 1998 an estimated one million violent crimes were committed against intimate partners (Rennison and Welchans 2000). The justice system has responded to this crisis by developing specialized court processes to handle domestic-violence cases. These courts, which are still in their infancy, vary widely in their structure and goals (Keilitz 2000). One court that has received national attention was implemented in 1996 in Brooklyn, New York, by the New York State Unified Court System in partnership with the Center for Court Innovation.

The Brooklyn Domestic Violence Court was designed to promote swift and certain responses to domestic-violence offenders while also ensuring the victim's safety. Defendants must appear regularly in the court, where they are subject to ongoing monitoring of court-ordered programs, such as batterers' intervention programs and compliance with orders of protection. Defendants remain account-able to and continue to appear in front of the same judge, even after case disposition and during the term of probation. A resource coordinator helps the judge monitor compliance by obtaining information from the district attorney, the department of probation, and batterer's programs. A victim advocate, who works in partnership with the prosecutor, ensures that victims have a safety and housing plan and are linked to counseling and other social services.

Another successful domestic violence court can be found in Lexington County, South Carolina. Gover, Brank, and McDonald (2007) found that the success of the court appeared to result from the emphasis on procedural justice principles. Victims and defendants were provided opportunities to participate in the judicial process and they reported high satisfaction with the operation of the court and the sentences pronounced. Procedural justice examines the processes and not just the outcomes of a case. The idea of procedural justice is based upon the concept that processes have a very strong effect on the way people obey the law. Paternoster, Bachman, Brame, and Sherman (1997) suggested that the subsequent behavior by the offender was affected more strongly by the manner in which the sanctions were imposed than by the sanctions themselves. It has also been recognized that punishment can create unintended results if it is inappropriately administered. Resentment and anger can occur if the person punished is demeaned, embarrassed, or diminished.

In the Lexington County court the judge and prosecutor communicated regularly and sentencing recommendations made by the prosecutor were more often accepted by the judge due to the collaboration. Observations and surveys conducted by Gover, Brank, and McDonald (2007) revealed that 90 percent of the victims and 68 percent of the defendants felt that the court gave adequate time to explain their side of the story, 77 percent of victims and 68 percent of defendants believed the outcome of their case was fair and just, and 67 percent of victims and 58 percent of defendants thought at the Lexington County domestic violence court's response to domestic violence cases was just right. It appears that the use of alternative dispute resolutions and emphasis on rehabilitation and treatment had positive effects on both victims and defendants. According to the researchers, the emphasis on collaboration between the judge, prosecutor, victim advocate, mental health counselor, sheriff's investigators, victim, and defendant led to a significant reduction in rearrests for domestic violence offenses. The court also established an active approach to addressing domestic violence that emphasized victim safety, offender accountability, and batterer treatment.

Domestic-violence courts provide a critical step in a continuum of response that begins with local police intervention and continues through ongoing community correction monitoring of the offender and community-based services for victims. As can be seen, when courts become more collaborative with professional outside of the courtroom workgroup the results become more beneficial for the victim, the offender, and the community.

Mental health courts

The creation of mental health courts is a recent action that creates collaboration between the criminal justice system and mental health professionals to address the needs of mentally ill persons who have been charged with non-violent crimes. Because of decreased funding in the area of mental health, persons suffering mental illness who commit non-violent crimes are placed in the criminal justice system instead of treatment facilities or programs. The criminal justice system is not equipped to handle mentally ill patients and so they do not receive the proper care and are eventually returned to the community where they often offend again. This begins a revolving door cycle that does not benefit the criminal justice system or mentally ill persons.

Mental health courts are still few in number, only about 150 according to the Bureau of Justice Assistance. They are usually structured similarly to drug courts where professionals outside of the courtroom work group collaborate with the work group to establish individualized plans to address the needs of the defendant. Often mentally ill persons who are arrested suffer from homelessness, lack of family support, substance abuse, and lack of finances to seek appropriate treatment or medication. The work teams establish treatment plans and also provide monitoring and often financial assistance to assist the individual in staying on the plan and avoiding being arrested again.

The case study that follows chronicles the establishment of a mental health court in a poor, rural area of southwest Georgia. Because most high-impact areas are in economically depressed communities, the success of this court is encouraging for those officials who work to implement community justice principles in deprived areas. Although the court was launched in a very poor area with few resources, it seems that the creation of such a court could be successfully accomplished in any jurisdiction, no matter the financial status, if collaboration between the courts and mental health professional is established.

Box 3.4 Albany, Georgia Mental Health Court case study

Because those with mental health issues often end up in the criminal justice system, Stephen Goss, a trial judge in rural southwest Georgia, started a felony mental health court. Judge Goss serves in an area where poverty is rampant and resources in the mental health field have been drastically decreased. The goal of the court is to help the appropriate agencies coordinate their efforts in addressing mental illness so that arrests and mental health facility stays are decreased and the overall health of the patient is improved.

Albany is a rural community located in southwestern Georgia. The population of the city is approximately 77,000 persons composed of approximately 68 percent African-American, 29 percent white, 2 percent Hispanic, and less than 1 percent Native American, Asian, Pacific Islander, and other races. The yearly median income is $29,000 for households and $33,000 for families, but the median income per capita is only $16,000. About 22 percent of families and 27 percent of the population were below the poverty line. Owner-occupied housing is one indicator of how healthy a community is and Albany has a 43 percent owner-occupied rate with 57 percent of the housing being renter-occupied. The national average is 67 percent owner-occupied and 33 percent renter-occupied so it appears that Albany is not particularly healthy in this area (US Census Bureau 2008). Overall, it can be seen that while the city has strengths, it also has a weakness in the economic conditions of the city and surrounding counties. The region is one of the poorest congressional districts in the country and has been designated as a federal health care professional shortage area (Goss 2008).

Judge Goss recognized that the criminal justice system had become the de facto mental health treatment center for many of the offenders arrested. Those with mental health problems who were arrested were not usually under the care of a health professional and did not have prescriptions to address their afflictions. These factors led to a revolving door process where the arrested persons were treated at the jails or admitted to mental health facilities where treatment costs were high. After the treatment the persons were usually given credit for time served and then released from custody. Because they had no support system at home, they would often relapse and be rearrested for violating the law.

A meeting including members from the local judiciary, law enforcement, jail staff, mental health professionals, and disability advocates was organized by Judge Goss. After that meeting and further discussion lasting several months, two needs were identified. The first was the need for better training for first responders such as police officers and paramedics and the second was to develop a systematic approach to court cases involving those with mental illness issues. The group recognized that the symptoms were being treated by the criminal justice system when the real need was to develop actions to address the underlying mental health and substance abuse problems of the offenders.

Judge Goss and the task force realized that a major factor in their problem was that the United States has moved from institutional-based treatment to more community-based treatment. While this move appears to be more humanitarian, there are some negatives associated with such a move. In many cases those who are placed in community-based treatment do not have stable living arrangements or family support and they often have financial issues that affect their ability to seek medical treatment and purchase needed prescriptions. Because of these unstable living conditions many of the individuals begin to self-medicate with street drugs or just cease looking for treatment options.

The group identified two general case scenarios that are usually experienced. The first is that the mentally ill person is in the community with outpatient counseling and treatment. In this scenario a stressor event occurs that overloads the ability of the person to cope with the stressor. The person may begin to act out, quit taking prescribed medication, increase alcohol consumption, and cease seeking professional treatment. Often the behavior to the individual becomes problematic enough that the police are called. When they arrive the individual may feel threatened and become combative leading to an arrest and entrance to the criminal justice system. In the second scenario, the mentally ill person is homeless. Here the mentally ill person lives on the street and often sleeps in doorways or other warm areas of buildings. When proprietors arrive the next morning they discover the individual and call the police. Officers who respond to the call usually realize the person has nowhere to go and often an arrest is made for loitering, entering the person into the criminal justice system. Many times those individuals arrested are gainfully employed but their incarceration prohibits them from going to work. If those individuals are receiving governmental disability payments the benefits are suspended because the individual is not working. It can be seen how this cycle can create financial hardship not only for the individual but the family as well.

Judge Goss also realized that many of the professions that are involved in this process are not accustomed to communicating with each other. He found that much of the problem stemmed from medical and legal professional being trained on confidentiality issues. He also discovered that very often the problem involved the lack of sharing information causing these professionals to be unaware of existing programs that could address the problem.

The program developed in Albany contains a court coordinator and two case managers on staff at the community mental health organization. Those staff members coordinate with jail nurses and help determine the appropriate actions that should be taken to address those mentally ill persons already in custody. The results have been a reduction in the jail population and medication costs to the county along with respect shown to the mentally ill individual.

In the postadjudication process, entrance into the court program is a voluntary process since being mentally ill is not illegal. If the person opts to participate in the program the treatment professionals make a recommendation to the judge and a case plan is tailored to the individual's needs. The probationer has an assigned state probation officer and a treatment case manager ensuring proper support mechanisms are in place. Borrowing from the drug court model, periodic judicial reviews are held to keep the judge informed on the progress of the individual and the need for any modifications to the treatment plan. Such hearings also allow the judge to praise an individual making progress and emphasize the need to follow the program to those who do not appear to be engaged in the process. It is also recognized that those with mental illness often do not have stable living arrangements because during their care they move from family member to family member. The program helps to stabilize these family settings so that the individual does not miss medication times or treatment appointments.

The program includes mandated participation in group or 12-step programs in cases where alcohol or substance abuse is a problem. There is also outreach to the community which generates support and material goods for those in the program. Local churches have provided clothing items for homeless participants and housing options have been developed through personal care homes operated by community organizations.

To assess the effectiveness of the program, administrators vertically studied the results of persons in the postadjudication felony probation program. The important issue examined is the number of times the participant has returned to jail or has to be admitted to an expensive in-patient stay at the mental health hospital. Administrators also look at a comparison of a participant's jail stays before coming into the program compared to after coming into the program. In a review conducted after the first 30 months of operation, it was found that 41 percent of the program participants were not rearrested after coming into the program. Participants in the program are felons and one of the positive steps has been probationers suffering from a mental health disorder only without a co-occurring substance abuse problem. It was also discovered that the probationers do well if living arrangements can be stabilized allowing them to have consistency in medication regimens.

Teen courts

Teen courts turn peer pressure on its head, using young people to censure teens who have broken the law. With the earliest documented teen court established in Grand Prairie, Texas, in 1976 (Godwin, 1996), teen courts have recently blossomed across the United States with 1,127 courts in 49 states (National Association of Youth Courts 2007). These courts, by providing an alternative to more formal case processing for young offenders, serve to craft a more meaningful response to low-level teen offending, as well as positively involve young people in the justice process. Teen courts fit into the rubric of community justice by creating a "community of teens" that work to promote and enforce appropriate standards of behavior for young people in their neighborhood.

Although there are many types of teen courts, in the basic model, young offenders who have already admitted their guilt to low-level offenses such as vandalism, truancy, shoplifting, and trespassing, participate voluntarily in a process in which their case will be heard by a judge and jury of their peers, who determine the appropriate sanction. Schools, probation departments, police, nonprofit agencies, and courts all may operate a teen court. Some teen courts use adult judges with youth juries and/or youth "attorneys," while other courts are fully staffed by young people. Typical sanctions might include community-service hours, essay writing, a letter of apology, service on the teen-court jury, and/or restitution. Teen courts may also work to incorporate family participation, with parents being required to take the stand or with mandated parental attendance at the hearing. Teen courts frequently draw on the principles of restorative justice by incorporating a social-service assessment of the young person prior to or after the hearing and subsequent linking to social services. One of the primary philosophical underpinnings for the use of teen courts is that youth continually cite peers as having the most influence on them as they are growing up. With this in mind, designers of teen courts argue that sentences pronounced by peers will have more of an effect on the future behavior of a defendant than a sentence pronounced by an adult who is seemly unconnected with the trial and tribulations of being a teenager.

The majority of youth courts rarely accept offenders with a previous arrest record, but it is known that repeat offenders tend to band together with other offenders to commit 50 percent of the juvenile crime (Forgays and DeMilio 2005). Forgays and DeMilio studied the Whatcom County Teen Court Program in Bellingham, Washington which did take repeat offenders into their program and found that through a cohort comparison found that recidivism was not a problem.

The researchers attribute much of the success of the program to the restorative justice principles on which it was founded. The important fact to be gleaned from the study is that it appears that inclusion of multiple offenders into a teen court program can yield success.

The most common evaluations of teen courts focus on the recidivism of the young offender, which disregards the multiple functions teen courts fulfill. These recidivism analyses fail to indicate a clear connection between lowered recidivism and teen-court participation. A recent summary (Butts and Buck 2000) of studies of youth courts found inconsistent results from recidivism analyses: some supported the idea that teen courts are more successful than regular juvenile courts, and others found no differences between the two in overall outcome. However, teen courts also serve to make justice processing more accessible to communities, to provide a community-based forum for the handling of youth crime, to increase public awareness of the legal system, to teach young people about the justice system, and to help young people feel responsible for their neighborhoods. The realization of these last goals will serve the most valuable community justice function by planting positive seeds in the community that will grow into increased community engagement in overall public safety.

Box 3.5 Red Hook Youth Court

Dave sits facing a jury of ten at-risk neighborhood youths all wearing Red Hook Youth Court T-shirts in a basement of a local church. The community advocate has already made an opening statement about the harm done to the community by Dave's recent truancy, mentioning that Dave not only is jeopardizing his own future but has also set a bad example for other young people in the neighborhood. The youth advocate has also made an opening statement stressing that Dave is generally well behaved and promises not to do it again. The judge just opened the questions to the jury. In a free-style manner, the jurors start asking about Dave's life – what he does instead of going to school, what he likes and doesn't like about school, how his relationships are with his family. During the course of their wide-ranging questions, they discover that Dave is frequently truant, that he smokes pot at home when he's not at school, and that he really likes art but doesn't like his teachers. Upon finishing their questions, the jury exits to deliberate and returns with a sanction that incorporates a letter of apology to Dave's mother, a drug assessment, and a goal-setting workshop. Several weeks later, some of the jurors talk about seeing Dave in the neighborhood asking how he is doing, and one juror said that he took Dave to his after-school art class. After completing their six months of service, many of the jurors mention that they feel more responsible for their neighborhood and will stop other kids when they see them writing graffiti or doing other vandalism.

Re-entry courts

Re-entry courts take the drug-court model of intensive court monitoring, therapeutic jurisprudence, graduated sanctions and rewards, and the combination of services with justice case processing and then apply it to offenders returning to the community from extended stays in jail or prison. Their goal is to stabilize parolees and probationers in the community when they first exit prison so as to prevent future recidivism. Recently spearheaded by an Office of Justice Programs initiative, there are only a few re-entry courts extant, with a handful more still in development. Although still too new to evaluate, re-entry courts hold the promise of alleviating the pressures of one of the fastest growing prison populations across the United States: technical parole violators.

Even though models of re-entry courts differ, they tend to combine similar elements. Offenders are assessed prior to release, at which point a re-entry plan is developed. Once released, the offender appears in a "court" established in partnership with parole or probation, which is often headed by a magistrate or administrative law judge rather than a sitting judge, because the offender's case has already been adjudicated. At the court, the offender is mandated to attend appropriate social and drug-treatment services, be law abiding, and engage in education or employment training. The offender will return frequently to court for parole and judicial monitoring and will be subject to a graduated system of sanctions and rewards in response to compliance with the court's mandates.

Re-entry courts may be located in a downtown courthouse, but they necessarily concern themselves with the successful reintegration of offenders into their home communities. To achieve this, the courts must draw on neighborhood-based community supports, which might include community-based social-service agencies, family networks, or faith-based institutions. Ideally, in drawing on these informal community institutions, re-entry courts will also serve to strengthen them, improving future prospects for overall public safety in the neighborhood.

The community court movement is at the center of tension that surrounds the idea of community justice. Do concerns about rights or concerns about justice take priority when they are in conflict? In practice, community courts are splitting the difference. The concern for rights during the adjudication process still predominates in the courtroom, while a concern for justice is gaining preeminence during the sanctioning process. One important reason for the increasing concern for justice during the sanctioning process is that the argument for rights has become steadily weaker as the cumulative effects of individual sanctioning decisions have become more apparent. In communities where people suffer poverty, substandard education and health services, and few economic opportunities, the same sanctions given to offenders add up to a more disproportionate impact on the community and the individual than they do in communities characterized by more resources and healthier community well-being. Despite continuing and prospective conflicts, community courts are showing that a fair balance can be struck between individual rights and community justice.

Box 3.6 Multicultural community justice

One of the promises of community justice is its ability to be responsive to cultural and racial differences among community residents. For community police it might mean looking at a group of people hanging out in front of a building not as potential drug dealers, but as community members seeking companionship and cooler air outside cramped apartments. For community defenders it might mean treating a client as a member of an elaborate family network who will not make decisions about the case without considering the needs of this network. Community mediators must regularly grapple with racial and cultural differences as they facilitate the direct communication of parties in conflict. Mediators must be adept at helping parties understand each other through a fog of disparate communication styles. They must also be sensitive to the role that racism can play in initiating and escalating conflicts and then in inhibiting the fair and reasonable resolution of conflict (Umbreit and Coates 2000).

Suggested web sources for readers:

National Association of Drug Court Professionals – www.nadcp.org
National Association of Youth Courts – www.youthcourt.net
Center for Court Innovation – www.courtinnovation.org
National Council of Juvenile and Family Court Judges – www.ncjfcj.org

References

Allen, F., 1996. *The Habits of Legality: Criminal Justice and the Rule of Law.* New York: Oxford University Press

Bazemore, G. and Umbreit, M., 2001. "A Comparison of Four Restorative Conferencing Models," *Juvenile Justice Bulletin* (February). Washington, DC: US Department of Justice, Office of Justice Programs, Office of Juvenile Justice and Delinquency Prevention.

Butts, J. A. and Buck, J., 2000. "Teen Courts: A Focus on Research," *Juvenile Justice Bulletin* (October). Washington, DC: OJJDP.

Coates, R. B. and Umbreit, M. S., 1999. *Research & Resources Review: Victim Offender Mediation Empirical Studies.* Minneapolis: Center for Restorative Justice & Peacemaking, University of Minnesota.

Conner, R. and Griffin, P., 1998. *Community Safety Law: An Emerging Legal Specialty.* National Institute of Justice.

Cullen, F. and Gendreau, P., 1989. "The Effectiveness of Correctional Rehabilitation: Reconsidering the 'Nothing Works' Debate" in L. Goodstein and D. MacKenzie (eds) *American Prisons: Issues in Research and Policy.* New York: Plenum.

Forgays, D. K. and DeMilio, L., 2005. "Is Teen Court Only Effective for 1st Time Offenders?" *International Journal of Offender Therapy and Comparative Criminology* 49, pp. 107–18.

Godwin, T., 1996. *Peer Justice and Youth Empowerment: An Implementation Guide for Teen Court Programs*. Lexington, KY: National Highway Traffic Safety Administration and the American Probation and Parole Association.

Gorczyk, John F. and Perry, J. G., 1997. "What the Public Wants from Corrections," *Corrections Today* (September).

Goss, S. S., 2008. "Mental Health Courts in Rural and Nonaffluent Jurisdictions," *Criminal Justice Review* 33(3), pp. 405–13.

Gover, A., Brank, E., and MacDonald, J., 2007. "A Specialized Domestic Violence Court in South Carolina: An example of procedural justice for victims and defendants," *Violence Against Women* 13(6), pp. 603–26.

Gray, K. B., 2008. "Community Prosecution: After two decades, still new frontiers," *Journal of the Legal Profession*, 32.

Herman, S., 2000. "Seeking Parallel Justice: A New Agenda for the Victims Movement," speech given at the National Press Club luncheon, December 15, Washington, DC.

Karmen, A., 2010. *Crime Victims: An introduction to victimology*. Belmont, CA: Wadsworth Cengage.

Keilitz, S., 2000. *Specialization of Domestic Violence Case Management in the Courts: A National Survey*. Williamsburg, VA: National Center for State Courts.

National Association of Youth Courts 2007. Available at www.youthcourtnet.com/content/view/35/49 [Accessed November 18, 2009].

Nugent, H. and McEwan, J. T., 1988. *Prosecutors' National Assessment of Needs*. Washington, DC: National Institute of Justice, US Department of Justice.

Office for Victims of Crime. 2000. *New Directions from the Field: Victims' Rights and Services for the 21st Century, Strategies for Implementation*. Tools for Action Guide Series: Training Manual. Washington, DC: US Department of Justice.

Ostrom, B. J. and Kauder, B., 1998. *Examining the Work of State Courts, 1997: A National Perspective from the Court Statistics Project*. Williamsburg, VA: National Center for State Courts.

Paternoster, R., Bachman, B. R., Brame, R., and Sherman, L. W., 1997. "Do Fair Procedures Matter? The Effect of Procedural Justice on Spouse Assault," *Law and Society Review* 31, pp. 163–204.

Rennison, C., and Welchans, S., 2000. Bureau of Justice Statistics Special Report: *Intimate Partner Violence*. Washington, DC: US Department of Justice, Office of Justice Programs, Bureau of Justice Statistics.

Spangenberg Group, 2001. *Keeping Defender Workloads Manageable*. Washington, DC: US Department of Justice, Office of Justice Programs, Bureau of Justice Assistance.

Thomson, D., 2009. "Substantially Reduce Mass Incarceration by Sentencing Focused on Community Well-Being," in Natasha A. Frosr, N. A., Freilich, J. D., and Clear, T. R. (eds) *Contemporary Issues in Criminal Justice Policy: Policy Proposals from the American Society of Criminology Conference*. Belmont, CA: Cengage/Wadsworth.

Tonry, M., 1993. "Sentencing Commissions and their Guidelines," *Crime and Justice* 17.

Umbreit, M. and Coates, R., 2000. *Multicultural Implications of Restorative Justice: Potential Pitfalls and Dangers*. Washington, DC: US Department of Justice, Department of Victims of Crime.

United States Census Bureau, 2006–8 American Community Survey. Available at www.census.gov/acs/www/ [Accessed November 30, 2009].

von Hirsch, A., 1993. *Censure and Sanctions*. Oxford: Clarendon Press.

Zedlewski, E. M., 1987. *Making Confinement Decisions*. Washington, DC: US Department of Justice.

Further reading

Courts culture and caseload

Eisenstein, J., and Jacob, H., 1977. *Felony Justice: An Organizational Analysis of the Courts.* Boston: Little, Brown. Still the best description of the social organization of the courts and how it affects court processes.

Harlow, C., 2000. *Defense Counsel in Criminal Cases.* Washington, DC: Bureau of Justice Statistics.

Lewis, C. S., 2001. *The Abolition of Man.* San Francisco: Harper.

McCoy, C., 1993. *Politics and Plea Bargaining: Victim's Rights in California.* Philadelphia: University of Pennsylvania Press. An analysis of the ways court culture affected the implementation of victims' rights in California

Rosset, Arthur, and Cressey, D. R., 1976. *Justice by Consent.* Philadelphia: Lippincott. Classic study of the way the courts' caseload affects court processing.

Sentencing reform

Byrne, J. M., Lurigio, A. J., and Petersilia, J., 1992. *Smart Sentencing: The Emergence of Intermediate Sanctions.* Newbury Park, CA: Sage. A description and evaluation of various alternatives to incarceration.

Griset, P., 1991. *Determinate Sentencing: The Promise and Reality of Retributive Justice.* Albany: SUNY Press. A critical assessment of the determinate sentencing movement.

Tonry, M., 1996. *Sentencing Matters.* New York: Oxford University Press. An explanation and analysis of contemporary issues in sentencing in the United States.

Innovation in the courts

Feeley, M., 1983. *Court Reform on Trial: Why simple solutions fail.* New York: Basic Books. A special report on the reasons why court reform in the United States has not succeeded in improving court performance.

Shapiro, M., 1986. *Courts: A Comparative and Political Analysis.* Chicago: University of Chicago Press. A classic description of various court systems and the social and political issues they raise.

Stone, C., 1996. "Community Defense and the Challenge of Community Justice," in the National Institute of Justice Journal, *Communities: Mobilizing Against Crime, Making Partnerships Work.* August.

4 Corrections and community justice

Compared to law enforcement and the courts, the correctional function has been a latecomer to community justice. As Chapter 3 indicated, community-oriented policing activity has a long history but did not become a core aspect of American policing until the 1980s; community-based courts have had a long tradition in America, but the community court movement did not gather momentum until the early 1990s. Corrections, by contrast, has begun to embrace community justice ideas only very recently.

Correctional operations are generally grouped into two types: (1) institutional corrections and (2) field-service corrections. Institutional corrections encompass jails (usually locally run by the city or county and where defendants await the disposition of their cases or serve short sentences of incarceration), prisons (usually run by states and where offenders serve longer-term sentences), and federal penitentiaries (where offenders convicted of usually more serious federal crimes serve the terms of their sentence). In contrast, field-service corrections usually encompass two sorts of activities carried out by two types of agencies. Probation is a nonincarcerative form of community supervision that is often understood as an alternative to jail (in some jurisdictions, a probation sentence is termed a suspended jail sentence). Parole is a form of community supervision that is meant to monitor the reintegration of offenders into their home communities as they return from prison.

This late arrival of the corrections field to the community justice arena is understandable, yet also ironic. It is understandable because to most people, the correctional functions call forth the imagery of prison and jail, and these seem to have a problematic relationship to everyday community life. Yet there is an irony because the most commonly used forms of corrections occur in the community (probation, parole, and community corrections), and these aspects of correctional activity would seem to be naturally related to the ideals of community justice. As we will see, correctional activity has a historical focus on individual offenders that makes a community justice orientation difficult to sustain, and this is as true for community as for institutional correctional strategies.

Even though correctional leaders have come late to the community justice scene, there is now an energetic interest in the way community justice principles apply to essential correctional tasks. In this chapter, we begin with a brief review of traditional correctional services. We then explore community justice in the correctional setting, and we describe ways in which correctional services are changing to incorporate community justice ideas. We conclude with a description of the challenge of community justice for correctional functions.

Themes in traditional correctional services

Many volumes have been written about corrections, and we must simplify a broad, complex topic to come up with a handful of themes that characterize traditional correctional activity. We summarize traditional themes to provide a starting place for talking about community justice versions of corrections in contrast to traditional corrections. The five themes we describe are dominant topics in traditional correctional thought, but they also have relevance to community corrections. In the latter case, they emerge not as core ideas, but as subtopics within larger concerns.

Offender management

In traditional corrections, the technical core is developed to manage offenders through the process of criminal sanctions. Correctional workers are held accountable for the way they deal with individual offenders. Computerized information systems track offenders from the point they are sentenced by the judge to the point they are terminated from correctional programs. Indeed, every aspect of correctional activity is designed with regard to the way it assists correctional workers in managing the offenders assigned to their care.

The offender-management theme determines the level of focus of correctional attention to be on the individual offender, not the community, the victim, or the system. The offender orientation permeates correctional action: institutional officers are assigned to work cell ranges or housing units populated by individual offenders, and they are accountable for what happens to (and is done by) those offenders; community supervision is organized into caseloads that are collections of offenders, perhaps grouped depending upon the way a classification system suggests they be handled. Under correctional authority, offenders are processed through stages of correctional work – pretrial, postconviction, and community re-entry. The meaning of corrections is operationalized by the way each of its clients is dealt with by correctional staff.

Risk

The central concern correctional officials emphasize in managing offenders is their risk. High-risk offenders are treated one way – managed with care and with an emphasis on control; and low-risk offenders are dealt with in another – given less restrictions and controls. Average-risk cases fall in the middle. Most correctional programs enable the risk assessment of a given offender to change as he or she is managed through the penal process, so that an offender-management strategy of tight controls may be followed by a much less restrictive approach as the offender demonstrates through behavior that risk is less than the close control requires.

Risk permeates correctional thinking. When a case fails, especially when a new crime is committed by a person under correctional authority, questions usually follow about why the risk was not anticipated. This means that it is unwise to underestimate risk, and correctional officials are encouraged to treat any risk indicator as important. At the same time, however, there are far too many cases under correctional control to allow them all to be handled as high risk. Correctional leaders are therefore caught in a bind – they have to find a substantial body of low-risk cases that justify diverting their attention to the more problematic cases. But whenever there is a problem with any of these cases, correctional officials are made to answer for not anticipating the risk.

Treatment

The idea of rehabilitation has received less support in recent years than it did for most for the twentieth century, but the idea of correctional programming is still very important. Almost all offenders have significant personal problems that, left unchanged, bode poorly for subsequent adjustment to community life after correctional authority ends: drug abuse, poor impulse control, lack of job skills, educational deficits, and so on. All correctional settings are asked to assess offender needs for treatment and provide basic programs that meet those needs.

Unfortunately, the success of correctional treatment programming is notoriously poor. It is not so much that "treatment doesn't work," but rather that even the best treatment programs work for only some of the clients, and all treatment programs have some failure. There is no "silver bullet" in correctional rehabilitation. Treatments are at their most successful when they address the needs of high-risk (rather than low-risk) clients, so we can see that treatment programming poses an inherent dilemma for corrections: the treatments are all going to have failures, and if they are applied correctly (to high-risk cases) to start with, they will have a larger number of failures overall.

Surveillance and control

Traditional correctional programs have a basic concern for safety of the community. This implies the need for a minimum level of surveillance and control and suggests that as program failures mount and as risk levels of clients get higher, the need for surveillance and control also increases. For correctional administrators, there are no excuses for losing control of cases. A basic requirement is to know where a client is supposed to be and to know if the client is actually there. Institutional correctional officials do counts several times a day to ensure surveillance and control, and community corrections workers employ home visits and drug testing to achieve similar knowledge.

With the advent of new technologies, the emphasis on surveillance and control has grown in recent years. From electronic monitors that identify a person's whereabouts to drug screens and lie detector tests, correctional officials now employ an ever increasing array of methods to assert control and aid surveillance. Whenever there is a problem in a particular offender's case, the question always seems to be, "Why wasn't this person's behavior under closer scrutiny?" It isn't possible to watch every offender all the time, but it is possible to give greater emphasis to watching particular offenders more closely, especially those of high risk or those who have complicated or significant treatment needs – in the former case, to make sure that the rules are being followed, and in the latter, to make sure the treatment program is working.

Punishment

If there is anything that citizens expect from corrections, it is that offenders will be sanctioned for their misconduct. This has two levels of meaning for correctional officials. First, it is assumed that correctional workers will make sure that punishments imposed by the court will be carried out as indicated by the judge. Second, when offenders fail to conform to the rules of correctional programming, there must be unpleasant consequences that will tend to persuade the recalcitrant to rethink their errant ways.

The metric of punishment has changed in recent years. Sentences are longer, correctional program conditions are more stringent, and expectations for compliance are higher than they used to be only a scant generation ago. This has caused some observers to consider punishment as the most important function of corrections. It is certainly true that the public's expectations of effective punitive approaches have been accepted by correctional authorities as an important force in the correctional agenda.

These five themes of traditional corrections – offender management, risk, treatment, surveillance and control, and punishment – form something of a modern language in the field. Any useful description of contemporary correctional policy will necessarily consider these issues. Yet they are not the dominant themes in community justice as it applies to the correctional arena.

Themes in correctional community justice

The strains of community justice call forth a different set of correctional themes. It is important to emphasize that these themes are different from those enumerated above, but not opposite to them. The most significant difference is that community justice seeks to align itself with and build the capacity of informal social controls at the community level. Formal social controls – police, courts, and correctional enforcement – are seen as of secondary importance in building a safer society than informal the social controls of families, personal associations, social organizations, and the private sector. Community justice recognizes the importance of the latter, and seeks to work with and through them to create a stronger community capacity for public safety.

Below we describe five community justice themes in corrections. We then discuss how community justice officials integrate traditional themes into the concerns emphasized by community justice proponents.

Neighborhoods and communities

Under a community justice model, corrections maintains a focus on neighborhoods and local communities. This focus stems from recognition that neighborhoods are a central aspect of contemporary life, and the correctional responsibility for public safety requires treating neighborhoods as a client. That is, the community justice model is not merely about the offenders assigned to correctional supervision and control, but is also concerned with the places where those offenders live and work and the people with whom they live and work.

The importance of neighborhood and community is straightforward for correctional functions that operate when the offender is residing in the community, such as probation and parole. The activity of these clients has enormous significance for community life, especially in relation to their struggle to remain crime-free. Beyond public safety, the presence of offenders in the community connects to the circumstances of many other residents, as offenders are also family members, employees, neighbors, parents, peers, and friends to those around them. As we pointed out in Chapter 1, the concentration of offenders in some locations is great enough that correctional authorities may have a role in the lives of a large percentage of people living there.

But the neighborhood connection also applies to the institutional correctional function. Communities comprise interwoven connections of interpersonal social networks. These social networks are the basis for collective community activity – it is through the social networks that groups form, resources are shared, and supports are provided. Criminologists agree that informal social controls form the basis for public safety in community life: the capacity of a community to achieve a degree of public safety through collective activity is referred to as collective efficacy (Sampson, Raudenbush, and Earls 1997). Without strong, broad networks, there is little collective efficacy.

Every time an offender is removed from the community for incarceration, those networks are affected. Whatever that person was doing that damaged the capacity of the network to support those enmeshed within it is eliminated by incarceration, but whatever that person was doing to assist the networks is also eliminated. Likewise, when an offender re-enters the community from prison or jail, those networks are called upon to absorb the person back as a resident. Thus, high rates of incarceration can become significant forces in the capacity of social networks in these communities to perform their public safety functions (Sampson, Raudenbush, and Earls 1997). When large numbers of men are locked up from a particular area, their children lack male supervision and their parental partners are forced to do double duty as financial and personal supports for those youngsters. When many residents are fresh from prison or jail, an area is forced to develop its informal capacities in the face of a large concentration of people struggling in the workforce and under close law enforcement scrutiny.

For these reasons, correctional functions under a community justice approach are concerned with particular neighborhoods and the people who live there. The issue concerns not only how an offender is behaving, but also how that offender's situation – in or out of prison – affects the people who are not under correctional authority.

Partnerships

Community justice organizations, including correctional agencies, do not work in isolation. Those organizations responsible for a special set of objectives, such as public safety, partner with other organizations to carry out their functions. The reasons for partnerships are fairly simple: the problems of community life are so complex and so interconnected that working on one set of issues in isolation from the others is not likely to produce much overall change. When organizations begin to work together, greater change can occur.

The most common correctional partnerships are formed with other criminal justice organizations, particularly the police. Under community justice, police become natural partners to probation and parole officers, and public defenders can work alongside correctional authorities to pursue the interests of the client – especially regarding treatment, employment, and family relationships. However, when it comes to forming partnerships in community justice, institutional corrections face the greatest challenge, but the idea that careful transition planning can improve re-entry success automatically suggests a role for community partners, even with institutional correctional functions.

Non-criminal-justice agencies also stand as good partners. For example, treatment providers become natural partners for the jail, as offenders prepare for release and seek to maintain continuity in treatment programming. Social services, such as welfare, child-protective services, and employment-related services, may also work closely with correctional activity under community justice approaches. Juvenile correctional workers align themselves closely with the schools. Overall, partnerships with nonjustice agencies are designed to encourage "seamless" service systems in which comprehensive strategies are concentrated in communities whose residents suffer from significant deficits.

Finally, community justice strategies seek private-sector partners. Among the most important partners are for-profit businesses that operate (or might operate) in the neighborhoods targeted by community justice initiatives. In making community quality of life a priority, community justice seeks to help transform troubled communities into places where businesses can succeed because this helps create employment opportunities (for offenders and nonoffenders alike) and bolsters a solid economic foundation for residents. In addition, community justice organizations build partnerships with private nonprofit organizations, such as foundations, to carry out community-development initiatives that build a firmer foundation for public safety.

Box 4.1 Operation Night Light

Operation Night Light began in November 1992 as a partnership between probation officers in the Dorchester, Massachusetts, district court and Boston police officers in the Anti-Gang Violence Unit (which later became the Youth Violence Strike Force). This alliance was created at a time when Boston was experiencing heightened gang violence, a rise in homicide victims under the age of seventeen, public alarm, increasingly bold behavior of gang members in courthouses, and criticism by minority community leaders and judges of police stop-and-frisk tactics. Probation officers worked independently of police, and curfews were not commonly imposed by the court and were difficult to enforce. In response to those problems, a few probation officers and police officers met informally to develop the Operation Night Light model as a more effective way of deterring juvenile violence.

Operation Night Light pairs one probation officer with two police officers to make surprise visits to the homes, schools, and work sites of high-risk youth probationers during the nontraditional hours of 7pm to midnight, rather than from 8:30am to 4:30pm, which was previously the norm. In Dorchester, where Operation Night Light started, probationer surrenders based on new arrests declined 9.2 percent between January 1994 and June 1996, compared with a statewide increase of 14 percent during the same period.

(see: http://ojjdp.ncjrs.org/pubs/gun_violence/profile33.html; accessed January 13, 2010)

Victims and communities

Unlike traditional justice services, community justice initiatives concern themselves with clients other than the offender under direct correctional supervision because the community justice agenda accepts responsibilities that go beyond the management of the offender. Community justice strategies recognize that crime and its consequences are profoundly important concerns for both victims and communities. For these clients, crime is a significant problem that needs to be overcome.

Traditional correctional practices will claim a concern for victims and communities that is indirect – by advancing public safety interests, traditional corrections indirectly benefit victims and their communities. Community justice embraces the interests of victims and communities directly. The problems victims encounter as a result of the crime and the difficulties encountered by communities resulting from the removal and return of resident offenders are made a part of the community justice agenda. The approach to these issues taken by community justice is one of problem solving.

Problem solving

Community justice is a problem-solving philosophy. The orientation contrasts with traditional criminal justice, which is adversarial. Under community justice, preference is given to amelioration of problems and long-range solutions to entrenched difficulties rather than the mere adjudication of legal disputes. This concern for identifying problems and finding solutions enables community justice strategies to embrace a concern for victims and communities.

The problem-solving orientation of community justice means that an unusual set of questions may be addressed by community justice through its partnerships. The community justice orientation allows correctional agencies to consider diverse questions: How do we occupy our youths' time in the immediate hours after school when trouble is so common? What can we do about all the trash along the streets of this neighborhood? How can we facilitate a neighborhood organization to deal with landlord–tenant problems? What can be done to decrease school truancy? What should be done about store owners' complaints about youth groups hanging on the street corner?

One of the reasons partnerships are so important to community justice is that problem solving is so important. Rarely are important problems simple. The important problems faced by communities and their residents are sufficiently complex that no single organization can resolve them in isolation. Therefore, the community justice orientation requires correctional agencies to reach out to other groups – police, social services, and the private sector – to fashion solutions to complicated problems.

Restoration

To some extent, every solution to the problem of crime involves some level of restoration because crime is destructive to society. It is destructive in tangible ways, as victims lose property and suffer personal injury. It is destructive in meaningful but less tangible ways, as citizens lose faith in societal institutions and residents isolate themselves from one another in order to remain safe (Zehr 1989).

This dual level of loss – tangible and social – suggests that restoration has two aims. One aim is to repair the losses suffered by victims of crime. This is accomplished by restitution, usually from the offender but often from the community as well. But the social damage of crime can be ameliorated only through social reparation. This involves offenders "giving back" to society by recognizing that the crime they committed was a wrong done, not just to the victim, but to everybody.

As an objective of community justice action, restoration replaces punishment at the top of the priority list. Community justice correctional action will include punishment, because community justice advocates recognize that one of the ways reparation is achieved is through legal sanction. But in selecting sanctions, there is often significant latitude, and, all else being equal, community justice strategies give highest preference to sanctions that restore the victim and repair the frayed social fabric that results from crime.

Box 4.2 Vermont restorative justice

The crime problem in Vermont is not the incidence of crime, but the fear of crime and the lack of confidence among the citizens in their criminal justice system. That fear has created a decade of increased reliance on incarceration as the dominant response to crime, and the corrections' budget has quad-rupled as education aid declines. As government has become increasingly centralized, a major source of citizen frustration is the inability to define what is being achieved by the justice system, both on an individual case basis and from the perspective of the community. As the media focus on the spectacular failures and the extremes of the spectrum, government is caught between overwhelming caseloads of minor criminals and the need to target resources to protect the public from the dangerous criminals. In the rush to efficiency, the government bypasses the most effective agents, the community and the family, instead focusing on the individual cases that squeak the loudest.

In the reparative probation program, ordinary citizens of Vermont make sentencing decisions about adult criminal offenders from their community. Board members meet with offenders and victims, resolving their disputes by providing the offenders with the opportunity to acknowledge their wrongdoing, apologize to their victim, and make amends to their commu-nity. The court sentences the offenders, having pleaded guilty to a nonvio-lent crime. The sentence is then suspended, pending their completion of a reparative agreement.

For the past 200 years, the fundamental purpose of sentencing and correc-tions has been retributive. For the past 100 years, judges have had only two choices in sentencing: to punish, or not. For the past 25 years, we have known that not only does punishment not work, but that it also makes most offenders more likely to reoffend. We have attempted to ameliorate the effects of punishment with rehabilitative strategies and alternative forms of punishment in the community. None of these has been spectacularly success-ful in reducing the demand for incarceration.

The reparative probation program represents a different approach. The boards are focused on the minor crimes – the "broken windows" in James Q. Wilson's phrase (Wilson and Kelling 1982) – the crimes that are too petty to be dealt with by the system and that both diminish the quality of life and are committed by criminals who learn that we do not care enough about their behavior to do anything about it. They are the crimes committed by our chil-dren and young people. Reparative boards give citizens an opportunity to do something about their neighborhoods and their communities. By involving citizens directly in decision making about individual cases, they are forced to look at the offenders not as strangers, not as numbers, and not as monsters. The offenders are forced to confront the reality of their offense and its impact on the community and their victims. This confrontation, with a restorative outcome, shifts the paradigm from punishment to reintegration. The offender is held accountable, the victim is restored, and the community is repaired.

Perhaps even more important, the dispute is resolved by the community, and the community is empowered. (see: http://www.doc.state.vt.us/gw2/ overview.htm)

Integrating traditional correctional thought into the community justice framework

The traditional concerns of corrections do not disappear under community justice; rather, they are incorporated into the community justice priorities. The most important of these priorities is the neighborhood and community focus of community justice, and most of the traditional correctional agenda is shaped by this orientation.

For example, *offender management* becomes community focused. The question is not how offenders may be processed through the criminal sanction, but how to best reintegrate offenders into the community. For this reason, community corrections apply most powerfully to the traditional activity of probation and parole, with more complex implications for institutional corrections. Because offenders live with their families and in relationships with their neighbors and others who share their context, the way offenders fit into community life is a concern of community justice offender-management strategies. Correctional workers become involved with key members of the offender's interpersonal network, and they also work to establish and strengthen new network ties – associates, organizations, and family members are important sources of support for reintegration.

In working with those in the offender's social network, community justice workers must bear in mind the *risk* the offender represents to people in that network and to others in the community. Building strong community ties cannot ignore the fact that offenders have shown, by their past behavior, a willingness to damage those ties through criminal behavior. Part of what makes working with offenders under supervision so complex and challenging is the need to balance a realistic concern for risk with the direct need to establish supports and inter-dependencies that are vulnerable to that risk. Community justice workers thus give a significant importance to the need to monitor the progress of those relationships, both to make sure that they are remaining supportive of continuing progress toward full reintegration and to pick up signals of potential problems that may put those networks at risk. Offenders can hardly be expected to achieve the aims of repairing broken relationships and restoring the costs of their past crime unless criminal behavior has stopped. And neighborhoods and communities have a legitimate expectation that offenders have desisted criminal behavior.

The two most significant ways that community justice workers ensure the progress toward reintegration is through the combined strategies of *treatment* programs and *problem-solving* efforts. Treatment programs control and reduce risk. Problem-solving strategies identify ways that risk may be overcome through new offender and community approaches. For example, an offender who has difficulty finding and keeping a good job can benefit from job-training programs, but these can be carried out in such a way that the offender earns some wages during on-the-job training in work that also benefits the wider community. Some of those wages can go to restitution, while some of the work can translate into community improvements, such as trash removal or housing renovation. Thus, community justice workers may try to develop on-the-job training programs that provide a beginning level of wages and include some degree of community service.

Finally, both *punishment* and *surveillance and control* are aspects of community justice, but they are used as tools to achieve eventual reintegration rather than as ends in themselves. By the fact that the offender is placed under correctional authority, punishment has occurred. Any losses of liberty (for instance, jail time or a prison sentence) and restrictions on freedom (through conditions of supervision) are deemed to be aspects of the punishment, and their imposition is the sanction for the offense. No additional sanctions need be imposed. By the same token, any surveillance or control that a case encounters is used as a means to facilitate reintegration. Surveillance and control are not seen as having value except that they are necessary to lead, eventually, to a fully reintegrated status for the offender. Risk levels, therefore, may dictate a need for certain kinds of surveillance or control, but these flow from special consideration in a case and the community, and are not a general part of the overall correctional program for every offender under community justice supervision.

Thus, under a community justice orientation, traditional correctional themes remain but are subverted to dominant, central considerations of community justice. It is possible to see indications of traditional correctional thinking when observing a community justice system in action. What is different is the larger and broader sense of client – including victims and the community – and the central concern for reintegration as the offender-management aim. Moreover, the question posed to assess the value of particular actions (Will this strategy help the offender adjust to the community more successfully?) is not directed mainly at the offender but is instead focused on the question of community quality of life (Will this strategy help strengthen this community and the offender's circumstances within it?).

How community justice changes the traditional correctional functions

The ideals of community justice can operate within traditional correctional functions, but they change the look of those ways of doing business. There are two main locations for corrections: the community and the institution. For each of these locations, traditional corrections has two types of functions: regarding the community, there are probation and parole (re-entry); regarding institutions, there are jails and prisons. This classification of correctional functions is a bit oversimplified, but it will enable us to consider the different ways that the concepts of community justice alter the tasks of corrections.

Community justice and probation

In many ways, probation is the correctional function ideally suited to incorporate the values of community justice. Probation (along with parole) involves community supervision, meaning that its operations occur in the community, and its clients reside in the community. Indeed, the phrase "community-based corrections," which denotes probation and parole functions, as well as residential community facilities, indicates the degree to which these functions have a natural relationship to the community.

Despite this seeming relevance to community, traditional probation has not realized a community justice orientation. In contrast, what most probation agencies practice is a form of "Fortress Probation" (Manhattan Institute 1999). Under Fortress Probation, the probation office is located adjacent to the courthouse, downtown, far away from the communities in which the clients live. Probation officers rarely visit clients in their homes or jobs, but instead see them in regularly scheduled visits to the downtown office. Caseloads are organized to make the reporting process easier: the caseload either has a balanced number of high-, moderate-, and low-supervision cases to make the workload of those cases manageable or has "specialized" clients representing particular problems or supervision issues (such as intensive supervision) to make management of those special requirements easier. Fortress Probation requires the clients to come to the office, report on their activities since the previous office visit, and provide a urine sample for testing to determine compliance with the restrictions on alcohol and drug use.

There are plenty of critics of the Fortress Probation approach. They point out that studies of probation effectiveness continually show the futility of the traditional caseload system of supervision (Manhattan Institute 1999), and they complain that the reactive style of Fortress Probation means that problems are not prevented but simply managed. One of the most significant criticisms of this traditional approach is that office-bound probation officers cannot engage in the kinds of community services that are needed to support adjustment to the community, and they fail to get to know anything meaningful about the offender's family, work circumstances, or living situation. Yet, these are the factors that will have more effect on the offender's eventual adjustment than almost any others.

Under a community justice model, probation moves out of the office and into community branch offices opened up in the neighborhoods where the majority of clients live, and probation officers operate from these neighborhood offices. Sometimes they work in the office, but more often they are in the community, working not just with offenders, but also with others who live and work in that neighborhood. The activities of the community justice probation officer go beyond mere supervision, but the strategy of community justice probation begins by locating the probation function in the places where clients live and work.

Being "in the field" makes it much easier for community justice probation to expand its correctional tactics and targets to include more than just supervision and surveillance of offenders under sentence of the court. The community justice probation officer recognizes that offenders often succeed or fail largely on the basis of the nature of informal social controls in their lives, and that probation can work to strengthen and augment those informal social controls. Informal social controls are the prosocial relationships that strengthen an offender's connection to a conventional lifestyle: family members, employers, associates, and community organizations. Probation can help enhance the role those informal relationships play in the offender's life by reinforcing their importance, supporting the offender's bond to them, and showing ways that they can assist the offender's adjustment.

A neighborhood-based probation system, therefore, does not concern itself with just the person on probation. It is also concerned with others in the neighborhood who might play a role in the offender's adjustment. Community justice probation seeks to build ties to various community organizations, such as neighborhood councils, social clubs, and churches, and it relies upon those various organizations to develop a better relevance to residents who are under criminal justice authority. Each of these targets can be a part of a probationer's "making it": business managers can become employers, churches can become support groups, and community organizations can become advocates for community services and even host them.

Community justice probation seeks ways to establish support systems in the community for probationers. Some offenders live in isolation, of course, and it is particularly important for probation to help these clients develop support in the community by turning to churches, civic organizations, and other community groups. But for most probationers, the key target for community justice probation is the family. When the offender's primary relationships are supportive of the offender's overall adjustment, chances of success improve. Family members do not automatically know what they need to do, however, so community justice probation officers can work with them to understand how they can help the offender succeed in the community.

Community justice probation is also concerned about victims of crime, as they are also residents of the community. In many cases, probationers are required to provide restitution to their victims, and community justice probation recognizes that ensuring restitution can go a long way to increasing community willingness to participate in this form of probation. From this perspective, the community is also a victim of crime, and offenders can be expected to make some form of restitution to the community, not just to the specific victim. Restitution to the community is usually some type of community service, such as repairing property, cleaning parks, or restoring damages in the neighborhood infrastructure.

By locating in the neighborhood, community justice probation tailors its efforts to the particular neighborhood. For example, if a location is struggling with truancy, community justice probation will work with police and child-protective services to develop truancy-prevention strategies, knowing that the children who are having the most trouble in school are often those whose older siblings or parents have been in trouble with the law. A place with a large population of elderly might develop a community-service system of delivering food and medicine to them, using the clients of the criminal justice system to make the deliveries. By accepting the responsibility to work on problems such as these, which extend beyond working with actual clients, community justice probation embraces a truly preventive function.

Often the public believes probation to be "soft on crime" and the offender merely receives a slap on the wrist. When probation is used properly it can be very effective in providing sanctioning and rehabilitation for the offender. The public desires sanctioning but they also want rehabilitative treatment to be included. Specific and general deterrence involve the offender perceiving that the cost of committing the illegal act (punishment) outweighs the benefits of committing the crime (reward). Spiegler and Guevremont (2003) argue that the criminal's perceptions about deterrence matter for rehabilitation and retribution. If the offender perceives the intent of the punishment prescribed by the sanctioning body not to be legitimate and deserved, the punishment received can lead to anger, resentment, and retaliation. In that case, deterrence would not be achieved because the punishment was not received by the offender with the proper intent. While offenders in general do not like to be punished, they respond to deserved punishment better than to punishment they believe is undeserved or excessive.

While probation does not provide the same level of sanctioning as imprisonment, it still does allow for some incapacitation due to the supervision provided by probation officers. Probation also allows for rehabilitative actions to be taken as well. Applegate, Smith, Sitren, and Springer (2009) studied misdemeanant probationers to determine their individual understanding of what the probation experience meant to them. They wanted to find out what goals each probationer thought probation was serving, not what goals the probationer believe it should strive toward. Applegate *et al.* found that the respondents thought probation was serving a variety of purposes, but a large number believed that their sentence was a deterrent and more than 90 percent of the probationers agreed or strongly agreed that they had given up any future crime so they would not be on probation again. About 60 percent felt that probation promoted personal growth and provided assistance with problems. Many respondents understood that their probation was serving a retributive purpose and more than half of the respondents felt their sentence was repaying society for their crime. Applegate *et al.* believe that it is important whether offenders perceive probation as a punitive experience. According to their findings a large majority of probationers perceive an increased risk for punishment for any future crime and say that the threat of probation will keep them from offending again.

While the study conducted by Applegate *et al.* only involved misdemeanant probationers, it seems reasonable that felons on probation would have some of the same reactions. One of the main reasons that the misdemeanant probationers felt they were being sanctioned was because they were being closely supervised by a probation officer who held their future in his or her hands. The message seems to be that probation, when administered properly, can provide the deterrence and sanctioning that the public wants along with the opportunity to rehabilitate the offender.

Box 4.3 Maricopa County neighborhood probation centers

The Maricopa County (Arizona) Adult Probation Department operates neighborhood-based probation services in the Phoenix area. Each service is a partnership between the probation department, the Phoenix Police Department, and community organizations in various neighborhoods. In 1996, the Maricopa County Adult Probation Department established its first neighborhood probation project in the Coronado district of Phoenix. Two other neighborhood probation projects soon followed. Neighborhood probation projects have two goals: to reduce recidivism and to expand the role of probation to include problem solving in the community.

Unlike intensive supervision programs, which define their target populations by offense, neighborhood probation partnerships define their target populations by existing neighborhood boundaries. For example, the Garfield neighborhood probation office targets all probationers living in the Garfield neighborhood of central Phoenix, an area a little more than 2 miles in diameter. Targeting established neighborhoods affords the partnerships easier access to community boards and churches.

Although each of the Maricopa County Adult Probation Department's three neighborhood probation partnerships adjusts its activities to fit the needs of its particular neighborhood, each shares several attributes. Each office maintains a strong relationship with local law enforcement. Informally, police officers spend time in neighborhood probation officers familiarizing themselves with probationers in the neighborhood and discussing cases with probation officers. Formally, police and probation officers coordinate roundups and probationers' participation in community-service projects. Police officers also provide backup for probation officers making home visits and aid in the observation and supervision of probationers, serving as an extra set of eyes while they are on patrol. In return, probation officers use their broader search powers to aid in police investigations, and police officers receive increased cooperation from the community because residents know they are working with probation officers.

Partnerships maintain a strong relationship with the community. Both probation officers attend all community board meetings. Probation officers and police officers coordinate projects in which probationers perform their community service in the neighborhood. Sometimes, maintaining a strong relationship with the community requires a deep understanding of the neighborhood. Staff from the Garfield neighborhood probation office regularly visit and provide services (such as running errands) for several elderly women in the area who are considered the neighborhood matriarchs. In exchange for these visits, staff receive valuable insight into the history of the neighborhood and the roots of any problems. Like police officers, community members often visit the neighborhood probation offices to talk with the officers about the neighborhood and its issues. Finally, each partnership maintains a strong relationship with probationers. Geographic proximity allows probation officers more contact with their probationers. In addition, probationers receive supervision from local law enforcement officials who are aware of their probation conditions. Because they are seen as part of the community, probation and police officers believe the contacts are more productive and that they have better rapport with the probationers. The community also assists in the supervision of probationers. Because probationers are heavily involved in community-service projects, residents see probationers performing valuable services for the neighborhood and, in turn, these residents are more likely to perform services (such as job placement) for the probationers.

The following example illustrates how these three functions interact. While attending a neighborhood board meeting in Coronado, probation officers learned that the biggest concern for the community was the condition of one particular home. The owner of the home had been accumulating garbage in his yard for years. Community members complained about its appearance and its odor. Further, they believed the condition of the home was responsible for lowering property values and for discouraging working families from moving into the neighborhood. Police officers explained that they would continue to issue citations, but they could not force the owner to clean his property. The newly established Coronado Neighborhood Probation Office volunteered to have probationers clean the house as part of their community-service obligations. The community board was thrilled and volunteered to provide extra equipment and labor, as did the local police precinct. The house was cleaned within a month. As yet, Maricopa County's neighborhood probation partnerships have not been evaluated. Nonetheless, officials believe the programs are meeting some of their goals. They note that there has been a 45 percent decrease in crime in Coronado, and that turnover is lower among neighborhood probation officers than among traditional probation officers.

Community justice and the jail

Most jails are community based in that they operate within the confines of a particular community, but turning a jail into a community justice correctional operation is not a simple matter. Jails handle offenders that are confined for various reasons: some are in lockup for only a night or two, until they make bail; others stay incarcerated until they are sentenced, then go to probation or prison to complete their sentences; still others receive jail terms as sentences and switch from being detained to doing time for a few months before they are released. Jails are very important to the community. There are almost 10 million admissions to jails each year, and a similar number of releases (US Department of Justice 1995). If the processes of removal and return are important to community life, then jails are a major part of those processes.

Most often, the typical jail inmate stays inside for only a few days or weeks and then returns to the community. What can be done about those cases from the perspective of community justice? Three principles would seem to be important in the application of community justice to the jail: informal social controls, transition planning, and restoration/restitution.

The jail stay, no matter how short, always represents a disruption in the offender's life, and the disruption can imperil the ties to informal social controls (family and others) that will prove so important after the offender leaves jail. If the person serves a reasonable period in jail – several weeks or a few months – there will often be profound consequences with regard to informal social controls and community supports: loss of a job, break in relationships, eviction from housing, conflict with intimates, and so forth. These can be quite problematic for later adjustment, even if they are very recent changes. A community justice orientation to a jail will try to minimize these losses. It will work to keep employment prospects strong, reach out to family members so they may retain contact with the person in confinement, assist community groups in reaching out to the jailed offender, and so forth. The broad aim of targeting these informal social controls is to try to create a situation in which the inmate, upon release, will be surrounded by supports that will tend to reinforce a positive adjustment. Perhaps most important, the jail staff can help set up treatment programs for drug and alcohol abuse or anger management that will continue to be a part of the offender's life after release.

Transition planning, therefore, is very important. In the typical case, a jailed inmate is simply released with no particular supports or assistance. In New York City, for example, inmates are released in the wee hours of the morning and put on a bus to the center area of the borough where they live. They dismount the bus into an awaiting gathering of drug dealers and prostitutes. Under community justice, the plan for return to the community – especially its impact on family, neighbors, and potential employers – is carefully factored into the way the release is conducted, and the idea is to use release as the first positive step in the overall adjustment to the community.

Jails can also play an important role in restoration and restitution. One of the ironies of incarceration is that offenders who are locked up cannot make restitution to their victims. But a community justice jail finds ways to make restitution possible: inmates are allowed to work for income that partly goes to a victim's fund, trustee programs are created that allow the offender to perform restorative services in the community, and inmate programs that benefit the community are encouraged.

The jail can also be decentralized to local levels, and facilities similar to halfway houses can be a part of the offender's initial stay in the community. These facilities enable offenders to work during the day, sustain their family contacts, and provide income to the family and restitution to the victim, all while becoming gradually more involved in the neighborhood and its system of informal social controls. Jails are not community-based correctional facilities, but they can be reconfigured to have a community justice relevance.

Box 4.4 Travis County community justice

Ronald Earle was first elected district attorney in Travis County (Austin, Texas) in 1976, after working previously in judicial reform, as a municipal court judge, and in the state legislature. Over two decades, Earle transformed the Travis County District Attorney's Office from a small office of about 10 attorneys to one that in 1996 employed 157 staff, including 57 assistant district attorneys, with a Felony Trial Division, a Family Justice Division (that coordinated the investigation and prosecution of child and family-related cases, and child-protection actions), and a highly developed Special Prosecutions Unit (that investigated and prosecuted public-integrity and fraud cases). During his entire time in office, Earle has seen himself – and acted – as a leader whose mission was to involve the community in criminal justice processes.

From early on, Earle led much of criminal justice planning and established many integrated initiatives among public and private agencies in Travis County and the city of Austin. For example, he wrote state legislation for and then helped to create a Community Justice Council and Community Justice Task Force, bodies that bring together elected officials, appointed professionals, and private citizens to oversee all criminal justice operations in the county. Along with his first assistant, Rosemary Lehmberg, who headed the Family Justice Division for many years, Earle was largely responsible for founding the Children's Advocacy Center in Austin. Here, as in other initiatives, the District Attorney's Office brought people in the community together, obtained support from the necessary agencies, helped find sufficient resources to get the project off the ground, and then when it became self-sustaining, passed it over to community control.

In 1996, Earle set up the first of several Neighborhood Conference Committees (NCCs), in which adult volunteers, cleared by Austin authorities and trained, serve on panels that hear cases diverted from juvenile court. After intensive hearings that involve the juvenile offenders and members of their families, the panels offer individualized contracts to offenders that include restitution, community service, counseling and/or treatment, and mentoring by adults in the community. Participating adults in the NCCs say they welcome the opportunity to take responsibility for directly addressing crime and working with juvenile offenders in their own neighborhoods. Anecdotal accounts of individual offenders' experiences suggest that one outcome of the

NCC process is the creation of strong relationships between the offenders and adults in the local community that survive the period of their contracts.

Earle ran for re-election against his first contender in 20 years. He used the campaign as an opportunity to inform the public about his record and the rationale that informed it. For example, he put forward a mission that included a commitment to fashioning criminal justice processes, including prosecution, in accord with principles of restorative justice. Within the District Attorney's Office, even the prosecution of cases was seen as an opportunity to help victims heal. Victim–witness advocates and assistant district attorneys work closely with victims throughout trials, and a number of programs, such as victim–offender mediation and restitution sessions, are available. Earle also pursues programs and processes that he believes will cause offenders to change their behavior, to take responsibility for their actions, and to make restitution. Diversion and treatment programs supported by the DA's office offer counseling, treatment and rehabilitative services, mediation, and community-service alternatives for both adults and juveniles. In 1997, a new Community Justice Center opened in Austin to house offenders from the local community and offer programs that would help them to work toward becoming part of the community upon release. Vigorous prosecution and punishment of offenders is secondary to, but accompanies, each of these goals.

Although Earle and his top staff in the District Attorney's Office have been involved for years in leading most of these efforts in the community, by 1998 they were engaging the entire office in sometimes heated discussions about changes that might be made to decentralize prosecution efforts and build accountability to local neighborhoods. Earle had hired a police officer experienced in community policing as program manager for a new "community prosecution" effort and was working with a new police chief in an attempt to build police–prosecutor collaboration by geographical area. He also moved into the area of quality-of-life offenses, publicly supporting an ordinance prohibiting camping in public spaces, designating assistants in the office to handle nuisance-abatement suits, targeting gangs and porn shops – all of which provoked considerable controversy and public debate. (see: http://www.ksg.harvard.edu/criminaljustice/publications/cross-site.pdf)

Community justice and the prison

Of all the correctional functions, the prison is the most removed from a community justice orientation. Yet prisons are an important part of community justice, even though they seem to be remote from community life. One reason is that each prisoner comes from a community, and concentrations of inmate populations often come from certain communities. On any given day, about 12 percent of the

African-American males in their twenties and early thirties are in a prison or a jail (US Department of Justice 2001); in some inner neighborhoods, such as in sections of Brooklyn, 15 percent of the adult males go to prison or jail each year (Cadora and Swartz 2000). These kinds of concentrations of removal (and return, which we discuss later) pose important issues for the communities in which the effects are most concentrated.

The typical prisoner is away from the community between two and three years. This is a long enough time to suffer severe disruptions in ties to informal social controls back in the community, and long enough to allow significant changes in the circumstances of those left behind. Children grow, spouses form new relationships, families move, loved ones die, jobs dry up, and society slowly changes in the technologies and everyday practices the released offender will encounter. For many prisoners, the seriously disrupted social ties are a major obstacle to overcome in the eventual adjustment back to the community.

Prisons can help make that process of adjustment easier. An emphasis can be placed on facilitating the maintenance of family ties through visitation programs and access to long-distance telephone services. (Currently, operator-assisted collect calls from prisons to home are among the most expensive calls in the industry.) Prisoners can receive the kinds of wages that enable them to contribute some money back to the family and to pay a portion of the necessary restitution as well. Inmates can also be allowed to interact with community groups and communicate with outsiders who might play a role in social supports upon release.

As the offender nears release, a process of planning for transition can occur. This process can help create linkages to the community by involving family members, employers, and residents' groups (such as churches) in the preparation for the transition. Prison time can shift to the community, as offenders move from the secure confinement of the remote facility to semisecure halfway-house facilities in transition neighborhoods. Treatment programs can be located in the community, and other supportive resources can serve both halfway-house inmates and community members equally.

The point of any community justice initiative in prison is to reduce the isolation of prisons from community life. Prisoners are being incarcerated because of their crimes, but with only minor exceptions, they will eventually return to the community. It is common sense to organize the incarceration term in a way that makes return to the community more likely to be successful.

Box 4.5 The Oregon Accountability Model

The Oregon Accountability Model is designed to provide efficient implementation of many of the Oregon Department of Corrections (DOC) initiatives and projects that provide a foundation for inmates to lead successful lives upon release. The Model has six components that are woven together to form a fiber that strengthens the department's ability to hold offenders accountable for their actions and DOC staff accountable for achieving the mission and vision of the department. The corrections plan is based on mitigating seven criminal risk factors that have been shown to predict future criminal behavior. The risk factors are associates, substance abuse, community functioning, education and employment, emotional and mental health, marital and family life, and attitudes.

The ultimate goal of the Oregon Accountability Model is to improve public safety. The program elements that work to address the previously listed risk factors are:

Staff–Inmate Interaction – Correctional practices such as classification, gang management, and housing assignment hold inmates accountable for their actions every day. It is recognized that staff interactions with inmates help shape positive behavior. The department encourages staff to influence inmates' behavior, acknowledge positive change and provide incentives to inmates to change their behavior.

Work and Programs – The Department of Corrections uses the assessments performed at intake to create a corrections plan for each inmate. The plan is specific to the inmate and is developed to prepare the inmate for living in the community upon release. Many correctional programs contribute to inmates' preparedness for work and others teach inmates job skills. Most Oregon state inmates have a job while incarcerated to give them on-the-job experience.

Children and Families – The department encourages productive relationships between families and inmates to strengthen ties and increase the likelihood of success upon release. The Children of Incarcerated Parents Program provides inmates with tools for successful parenting and allows opportunities for inmates to practice those pro-social behaviors.

Re-entry – The department is involved in a statewide project that focuses on transition – a seamless movement of offenders from the community to incarceration to community supervision. Connections with the community before release are important factors in offenders' success on the outside, and may include work, treatment religion, and housing. Seven of the department's prisons have been identified as reentry facilities and they will be geared toward preparing inmates for release during their last six months of incarceration.

Community Supervision and Programs – The department continually works in partnership with each county to develop, deliver, and administer best practices regarding supervision, sanctions, and programs for offenders and their families in the communities. The goal is to reduce the odds that these offenders will commit new crimes. (see: www.doc.state.or.us/DOC/PUBAFF/oam_welcome.shtml; accessed February 12, 2010)

Community justice and parole (re-entry)

Each year, almost 600,000 inmates are released from prison (Travis, Solomon, and Waul 2001), and their collective impact on the communities they re-enter is significant. Studies show that the rate of crime in a given community is associated with the number of prisoners returning to that community (Clear, Rose, and Ryder 2000). Obviously, community safety is an important consideration in the re-entry of offenders.

Community justice in re-entry can function in much the same way as community justice in probation: through a neighborhood center that provides an array of services to newly released offenders, their families, and other residents. Indeed, in most communities with high concentrations of offenders as residents, the re-entry services will be a part of the community justice neighborhood center operated by probation. Because the same sorts of relationships are needed with employers, social services, community groups, and victims as were described for neighborhood probation centers, re-entry services fit in with the approach of such a center.

The main additional function of a neighborhood-based re-entry center is participation in the transition planning process that begins with the last stages of incarceration. Family members, potential employers, and others are consulted in the release decisions and the circumstances of the offender's return. A discussion is held regarding the supports that will be used to maximize the opportunity for successful adjustment, and the responsibilities of the offender in re-entry are explained. The role of key people in the offender's re-entry is developed and mutually understood by the local residents and the offender alike. When re-entry occurs, everyone is prepared for it.

Box 4.6 Rhode Island Family Life Center

The Rhode Island Family Life Center is a collaborative project of the Rhode Island Department of Corrections and local community-based and civic organizations. In 1999, the project laid out a detailed plan for how it would merge correctional operations with community participation as described below.

Discharge Planning: The Family Life Center (FLC) will incorporate a strengths-based approach to case management, employing Community Living Consultants (CLC) in lieu of case managers. The CLC will first meet with the offender, who participates in the process voluntarily, to begin building a relationship through the discharge planning process 90 days before release. The CLC will spend time with the offender to create a workable discharge plan that capitalizes on the offender's assets while addressing any outstanding service needs. In this way, offenders will feel a sense of ownership over the process and will develop a relationship with the CLC that will be continued upon release. This early relationship building and buy-in will be the seeds that will grow into offenders' long-term engagement with the FLC. At the same time, the CLC will work with the offender to identify family members and other familial networks, which can serve to support the offender as he or she returns to the community. The CLC will reach out to these support systems to help prepare them for the offender's return and will also help address any service needs that they may have.

Case Process: Each CLC will handle approximately 20 to 30 active cases at any one time, taking in seven new participants a month. The most intensive engagement will take place six weeks prior to release and six weeks after release to the community. While the CLC will intake 40 cases a year, the natural flow of adjustment to the community and client attrition will allow for an active case load of 30 clients, with a much smaller number taking up the majority of the CLC's time. The FLC will house five CLCs who will retain a generalist perspective – understanding that offenders and their families have complicated lives that require holistic responses. The FLC's program coordinator will have the clinical expertise to assess offenders for mental health and substance-abuse services. The bonding relationship between the CLC and the offender is critical to the offender's successful reintegration, so CLCs will remain engaged with those offenders who are temporarily remanded. CLCs will meet weekly as a group with the program coordinator to review all current cases, share information, and ensure that offenders and their families are receiving the best possible care. CLCs will follow up with their clients for a period of 18 months in order to help them access services as new needs arise and to gather data that will help assess the efficacy of the FLC's interventions.

Offender progress in stabilizing in the community will be celebrated at quarterly ceremonies. Offenders who have maintained a period of stability in the community as defined by the commission – having no new criminal offenses and meeting the majority of their self-defined goals – are eligible to become alumni of the FLC.

Criminal Justice Partnerships: The FLC will have two on-site probation and parole officers who will be supervising offenders returning to the four zip codes. The community supervision officers will work as a team with the CLCs, holding regular meetings to discuss offenders' progress meeting their goals. Community supervision officers will work together with the CLCs to devise alternative responses to technical violations in order to help offenders remain within the community, rather than be remanded.

Social Service Partners: The FLC planning committee has selected five major service agencies to provide services to the FLC's clients. During its transitional phase, the FLC will develop Memoranda of Understanding with each of these providers. The following five agencies have agreed to provide services to offenders involved in the FLC: Amos House; The Providence Center; Phoenix House; The Urban League; and Miriam Hospital.

- Amos House is a multipurpose agency located in South Providence specializing in providing shelter for the homeless. It provides case management and a variety of social-service programs for this population and will support FLC participants through the provision of transitional housing and job-readiness training.
- The Providence Center will provide services for returning offenders who require treatment for mental illness, chemical dependency, behavioral disorders, and emotional problems. The Providence Center's services include medication, case management, and psychotherapy services.
- Phoenix House will provide substance-abuse treatment services for offenders at the FLC. Phoenix House runs a long-term residential therapeutic community and an outpatient clinic. Phoenix House has designed treatment specifically for Latino/Latina clients and provides counseling for youth at the Rhode Island Training School, the youth detention facility.
- The Urban League is a community-based nonprofit organization with a 62-year record of service to the Black and other minority populations in Rhode Island. Its mission is the elimination of racial discrimination and segregation and the achievement of parity for minorities. The Urban League has developed a special expertise in employment and training issues and will provide employment training and job-readiness training to participants of the FLC.
- Miriam Hospital will provide health-care services for returning offenders, who typically have health problems related to hepatitis C, HIV/AIDS, diabetes, and hypertension.

Community corrections and restoration

One of the values that sets community justice apart from traditional criminal justice is a concern for restoration. Crime is understood as impairing community. It damages the fabric of mutual trust that is necessary to the very idea of community, and it generates fear of association that makes community harder to achieve. Doing something to prevent crime is a part of building community, but doing something about the damage that results from crime is an essential part of community justice.

Community justice approaches restorative justice as problem solving. It is significantly different from the "contest" version of traditional criminal law, which is illustrated by the very name given to its cases: for example, *State v. Wilson*. By contrast, community justice conceptualizes a criminal case not as a contest between two disputants, but a problem between three parties: the offender, the victim, and the community. What is needed is a way to design case outcomes that best meet the legitimate interest of each party to the problem at hand.

In community justice, the offender has a legitimate interest in being allowed to find a way to re-establish ties to the community; the victim has an interest in having the losses suffered at the hands of the offender restored; and the community has an interest in developing some confidence that the offender will refrain from this kind of conduct in the future. Each interest connotes an obligation, as well. The offender is obliged to repair the damage and to provide some tangible assurance that criminality will not recur. The victim has an obligation to identify the losses that need to be restored and to entertain the possibility of a reconstituting community with the offender (note that this is not an obligation to rebuild community with the offender, just to entertain the possibility of this rebuilding under the "right" circumstances, regarding which the victim has a voice). The community has an obligation to identify the circumstances under which both the victim and the offender can be restored to community.

Restorative community justice is an important, different way to conceive of justice. It gives both the community and the victim an active role in determining the appropriate sanction in a case, and it gives the offender a voice in that same process. By opening the process to those who are most affected by its outcome, the restorative model seeks to develop solutions both to the problems that result from crime and to the impediments to community that accompany the existence of crime.

Women in prison

Much has been written about the effect of imprisonment on the fabric of the community. The continual movement of persons into and out of the community creates instability within families and the community at large. Often overlooked in that discussion is the effect of the imprisonment of women on families and the community. Because males are seen as income earners their absence can be quantified more easily than women.

From 2000 to 2006 the rate of females under state or federal jurisdiction exceeded that of males. According to US Department of Justice (2007), the annual growth rate for female incarceration in state and federal prisons was 2.9 percent compared with 1.8 percent for men. From 2005 to 2006, the change was 4.5 percent for females and 2.7 percent for males. It is clear that the increase in females being placed under state or federal jurisdiction presents many problems for the stability of communities, since women are the primary caregivers for minor children.

Women find themselves being incarcerated for a variety of reasons, but in many cases the arrests comes because of a boyfriend or significant other who uses the woman and her residence as a base for illegal activity. The relationship is often characterized by emotional abuse and the insistence of the male that if it were not for him, the woman would not be able to find companionship. Often the male provides just enough financial support for the woman and the children to allow her to stay at home and watch the "business" while he goes out to conduct illegal activity. In low-income areas the place of residence is often public subsidized housing or rental property and, when the illegal activity is discovered, the woman and her children are evicted. Once the eviction is completed the male usually disappears leaving the woman to care for the children with no stable place to live. If the evidence indicates that the woman was aware of or participated materially in the criminal activity, an arrest follows and children are placed in foster care or turned over to immediate relatives such as grandparents for proper care.

La Vigne, Brooks, and Shollenberger (2009) examined female prisoners leaving the Texas prison system and returning to Houston. They found that those prisoners who were mothers looked most forward to reuniting with their children after release but they also experienced more conflict with other family members when they returned home. The researchers also discovered that women had greater difficulty in finding a retaining employment for the first several months after release. This discovery was attributed to the fact that women are less likely than their male counterparts to have gained skills or participated in job training programs while incarcerated. In concert with previous research, La Vigne *et al.* found that the women in their study were more likely than men to have problems stemming from drug use and were twice as likely as men to be back in prison due to a drug offense or a property offense driven by addiction problems.

Some implications from the Houston study are that treatment programs should be revised to address women's issues and challenges holistically with attention toward the factors that drive women into substance abuse. The researchers also cite the need for educational and employment programs that assist women in finding legal employment after release. This factor is critical because many women released from prison are the sole breadwinners for their families and their lack of education and experience makes finding meaningful employment difficult. For both females and males released from prison, family relationships are critical to providing the necessary support for the prisoner to continue employment, refrain from using illegal substances, and reoffending. Research has shown that males are able to reestablish family ties with immediate relatives and significant others in their lives. Women, on the other hand, appear to have more difficulty in reestablishing relationships with immediate family and the researchers theorize that this tenuousness in the relationships may center on the minor children that have been cared for by the family during the prisoner's incarceration. La Vigne *et al.* recommend pre-release family conferencing where the prisoner and the family members can strengthen the family support systems but also share openly concerns all may have about the roles and responsibilities of each family member. These policy recommendations can be helpful to pre-release specialists in all state correctional facilities. Properly preparing the women for re-entry into society appears to pay benefits for not only the prisoner but the family and community as well.

Community justice centers in the neighborhood context: a vision for the future

As it stands, the prevailing criminal justice system is almost entirely focused on responding to individual crimes, prosecuting individual cases, and managing individual offenders. Despite the myriad experiments in community justice, taken as a whole, the criminal justice system – particularly corrections – is dominated by the individual case orientation and has not made a *systematic* shift toward organizing its operations around the circumstances of places. But what would corrections look like if it were systematically oriented to do business in neighborhoods? A common expression holds that "if you don't know where you're going, you probably won't get there." To that end, it is probably important to develop an anticipatory picture of how corrections might look if it were neighborhood based.

Although everyone's vision for community justice might not look the same, the community justice "movement" is at a stage in its development in which it can only benefit from a diverse set of ideas. We offer one, brief scenario of how a corrections system infused with the ideas of community justice might look in a particular neighborhood.

One way in which corrections might incorporate community justice principles is in the form of a neighborhood community justice center located inside the neighborhood, ideally in the hardest-hit area of the community. The center serves as a resource both for residents being supervised by corrections agencies and for their families, victims of crime, and other residents in need of assistance. To overcome the fragmentation of services that traditionally prevails between criminal justice agencies, the center houses offices for transitional staff from the state's prison system and local jail, supervision staff from the probation/parole department, and police officers from the local precinct. To facilitate working partnerships with the community, the center also makes space available for the local housing-development organization, substance-abuse treatment agency, local YMCA, vocational training and job-placement assistance program, victim-assistance agency, and other local faith-based or community social-service institutions.

In addition to the daily interactions that close physical proximity encourages, the center's staff meet monthly to assess progress in the neighborhood, identify new priorities, and plan how to implement its strategies. At the same time, the center serves as a meeting place for a variety of community discussions and forums. Residents under the supervision of the justice system report here, as do ex-prisoners making the transition back to the community; but other residents also use the center. When there are questions about illegal dumping or trouble corners, residents know that the center will help refer them to the proper authorities who can best address their problems.

While the center is a locus of activity in the neighborhood for community justice, not all the activities it sponsors take place there. Indeed, the majority of programs and activities, which are only planned and coordinated by the center, take place all around the neighborhood. These neighborhood programs include community guardianship, civic leadership, workforce development, and supportive health care and housing.

Community guardianship

The community guardianship program teams up probation and parole officers with local tenant associations, home owners, parks employees, and block associations. Together, they sponsor civic, recreational, social, and other community-service activities in areas of the neighborhood that have been identified as hotspots of trouble. Instead of depending entirely on police to respond to complaints by conducting sweeps and arrests, the guardianship program establishes proactive social events that make delinquency and other drug and public order crime difficult to take place. At the same time that it targets trouble locations, the guardianship program brings together mentors from faith-based and other social-service organizations, like the YMCA, and probation/parole officers. These mentor teams work closely with high-risk residents who are on probation/parole to ensure that they have the sufficient guidance and support to avert opportunistic illicit activities.

Civic leadership

The civic leadership program is a project-based series of neighborhood revitalization initiatives that combine obligatory community service for residents under probation/parole supervision and service by other residents who volunteer their time to community improvement projects. The civic leadership program brings together organizations like Habitat for Humanity, the local community-service society, public schools, local businesses, and the municipal parks agency with probation/parole and corrections officers. The coalition targets vacant lots, trash-strewn streets, broken-down and graffiti-covered storefronts, and dilapidated housing for beautification and rehabilitation. Resident volunteers are teamed up with resident offenders to create community gardens, murals, and other public-space projects with technical support from the participating agencies and supervisory services from corrections officers.

Workforce development

A priority of the community justice center is the financial stability and informal social control that comes from stable employment. The probation/parole department works in partnership with a coalition of local businesses, the community employment agency, schools, and public libraries. Together they offer vocational literacy, employment training, and job programs to both resident offenders and other residents in need of employment. Local employers are provided with tax credits for employing probationers and parolees. The local employment agency sponsors a job club to help employed probationers and parolees keep their jobs. They work with a probation/parole officer who offers specialized support around employment obstacles typically encountered by residents with criminal records. At the same time, job-skills training is integrated with vocational-literacy education and tailored to the kinds of jobs that the local businesses offer. These services are also offered to local residents who are in need of literacy services.

Supportive health care and housing

The center sponsors a stable housing program because it is well documented that one of the greatest impediments to crime-free living is lack of housing for returning ex-prisoners. Among the numerous housing initiatives sponsored by the center, two are of particular note. The first focuses on the eviction from public housing of family members who have a criminal record. To overcome this obstacle, the center brings together a coalition from its guardianship program and public housing officials to petition for exceptions to the public housing prohibition. The program recruits members of the tenant association and the mentor teams to sponsor the return of ex-prisoners to their former public housing apartments. In another of its housing programs, the center works with the local housing development organization to establish tenant-managed, affordable-housing apartment complexes. Through an innovative funding strategy, the center combines federal funding for housing with state correctional tax credits traditionally given to construction firms that build prisons, and use these funds to build supportive, mixed-use housing for low-income residents and residents involved in the criminal justice system.

Together, these programs provide only a glimpse of the possibilities that a community justice-oriented correctional agenda could accomplish if it became committed to these principles. The possibilities are endless, but these are some of the kinds of partnerships and coalitions that could arise if corrections shifts its attention from an exclusive concern for the individual to one that takes into consideration the community's priorities, needs, and inherent strengths.

Box 4.7 Returning home: understanding the challenges of prisoner reentry

In order to understand issues that contribute to the successful reentry of prisoners into society, The Urban Institute sponsored a 2009 study of 210 men exiting prison and returning to the Houston area. The study conducted three waves of interviews with the men (just prior to release, two to four months after release, and eight to ten months after release), conducted extensive interviews with family members of men being released from incarceration, and obtained information through semi-structured telephone interviews with community stakeholders to gather information about what factors make reentry successful. While the study is specific to the release of Texas prisoners who return to Houston, it provides insightful information that can be adopted by correctional officials and reentry specialists throughout the United States.

Male prisoners returning to Houston, Texas

Most of the exiting prisoners are African-American or Latino who are familiar with the criminal justice system through previous incarcerations. The study found that family support was a major factor in assisting the men with housing, financial support, and emotional support. Those men with higher levels of family support were also less likely to engage in substance abuse after release. Another issue discovered through the study was that the men left prison with a large amount of debt and they encountered challenges in finding employment due to the lack of photo identification and the existence of a criminal record. Unemployment and substance abuse are also key contributors to reincarceration. Prisoners who participated in substance abuse and employment programs in prison and community programs immediately after release in prison were less likely to return to prison. This finding suggests that prison and community programs can be effective if administered correctly.

The researchers found that after release, one-third of the prisoners wanted to participate in programs in the community but were not able to do so mostly because they were unaware of available programs. When asked what programs would be helpful after release the men responded with job training, health insurance, education, and financial assistance. Of interest to the researchers was that eight to ten months after release about one-third of the men reporting being involved in a community organization of some type, with the most common type of organization being a religious institution. It appeared that that maintaining involvement with religious organizations decreased over time with about 32 percent of the men who reported belonging to a religious institution during the first interview no longer belonging eight to ten months after release. The data indicated that belonging to a religious organization shortly after release was associated with lower incidents of substance abuse and lower incarceration rates and that those who left their religious organization at a later point lost the positive benefits of association with the organization and suffered a higher likelihood of substance use and recidivism.

The research findings suggest that those released from prison are lacking needed support both behind bars and after release at the basic level the men being released needed a picture identification that does not indicate they have been recently released from prison, appropriate clothing to wear to seek employment, and resources that sustain them and keep them from being tempted to turn to crime to obtain needed cash. Also problematic is the degree to which the released prisoners find residence in communities where drug dealing is the norm and opportunities for legal employment are scarce. Education, such as obtaining a GED or participating in job programs immediately after release, appeared to lead to employment for longer periods of time indicating that these types of programs should be enhanced and properly funded. It also appears that adding substance abuse treatment to these programs would help bring stability to the prisoners since substance abuse is a major factor in loss of employment after release. As previously discussed, support systems are very important in preventing substance abuse and encouraging employment stability. Men who were successful in their reentry tended to be those who had minor children, had supportive families, and had an affiliation with a faith institution. The message for corrections officials and reentry specialists is that important relationship ties can be strengthened through increasing opportunities for communication and visitation while men are in prison, as well as providing support for the families who provide financial and emotional support for those returning home.

Family members of returning prisoners in Houston, Texas

In this portion of the study interviews were conducted with family members of returning prisoners. For this study family was defined as "blood or legal relatives, people you have a child in common with, and significant others or guardians you live with before you entered prison or state jail this time" (Shollenberger 2009: 2). In this study the family members are typically female, predominately African-American, and older than the returning prisoner.

For many family members the release of the prisoner in this study was not the first time they had experienced such an event. Approximately 30 percent of those responding to the survey reported having at least one other relative incarcerated at the time the interview was conducted. As a result, most of the family members knew the processes involved with incarceration and reentry. Male prisoners returning home were able to nominate family members to participate in the interviews with researchers and they chose parents or grandparents first, followed by siblings and intimate partners. This differs somewhat from female prisoners who tend to choose children or grandchildren. Overall, the relationships between the family members and the returning male prisoners were strong and long-standing and the relatives had maintained contact with the prisoners during their incarceration.

According to previous research, contact with family during incarceration leads to positive outcomes for returning prisoners. Family members interviewed indicated that there were often barriers that interfered with their keeping contact with the prisoner. The barriers cited were distance, transportation, phone policy, prison/jail not in a nice place to visit, scheduling conflicts, visitation rules, and cost of visiting. Family members often indicated that the barriers of distance and transportation were often linked and ability to find transportation for a trip two or more hours was difficult to locate.

While the family members report that reestablishing relationships was not difficult, they did report difficulties such as increased anxiety, financial hardships due to adding financial support of the prisoner, other friends and family pulling away, trouble in other relationships, and returning relatives had previously stolen from them. They also report that they supported the prisoner in a variety of ways such as help with housing, financial support, finding work, child care, and substance abuse treatment.

When asked by the researchers what resources and support would be helpful for family members of returning prisoners the responses included the following:

Financial support: Family members expressed a need for financial support especially in the first few weeks after the prisoner returned. They felt that services such as food stamps, transportation vouchers, help with rent and utility bills, and clothing assistance for the prisoner would be very helpful.

Counseling: Some family members felt they needed emotional support more than financial support to help them cope with the reentry of the prisoner. They desired a range of counseling services such as support groups, mentoring programs for returning relatives, and family counseling.

Faith and religious support: Some family members said that faith, God, or prayer was all they needed to cope with the reentry process. Others cited a need for counseling or other resources to be faith-delivered through a religious organization.

Support for returning relatives: Many family members chose to focus on the needs of their returning relative and not on their own needs. Specifically, they believed job placement assistance, substance abuse counseling, mental health services, support groups, and mentoring by prisoners who had successfully reentered society would be helpful.

Community perspectives

Researchers conducted semi-structured telephone interviews with service providers, local advocates, and officials in corrections, parole, probation, policing, and city government to obtain community perspectives on prisoner reentry. They also conducted focus groups comprising residents of Houston neighborhoods with the greatest concentration of returning prisoners.

During the interviews, several challenges were cited by those interviewed. Community stakeholders believed that finding appropriate housing is a vital part of successful reentry. They believed that an increase in transitional housing could be helpful in providing some initial stability to the returning prisoner. The stakeholders also recognized that finding legal employment was also a problem because employers often discriminated against returning prisoners. It was suggested by the stakeholders that education of employers about tax incentives and bonding programs can support the effort to employ returning prisoners. In addition, they believed that providing education and skills training for the returning prisoner would make them more attractive to employers. Also recognized was the need for substance abuse treatment for reentering prisoners. The stakeholders recognized that treatment options are often lacking and funding of these options by private and governmental entities were often problematic.

The respondents recommended an increase in reentry preparation, education, skills building, substance abuse treatment, and counseling within the prisons. They also recognized the need to encourage and strengthen the family connections to increase the chance for success after release from custody. The stakeholders believed that preparing inmates for release should happen throughout the course of their incarceration, not just in the few months prior to release.

Many of the residents identified the lack of post-release supervision and support as a cause of recidivism. The residents believed that the supervision is improving but there is still a shortage of probation and parole officers to provide the necessary supervision.

The stakeholders also expressed an interest in seeing local elected officials becoming more aware of reentry issues and allocating more resources toward addressing the issue. In the area of nonprofit service providers the respondents felt that the social service infrastructure in Houston was underdeveloped, overburdened, and unable to meet the needs of the returning prisoners. They recognized the funding issue for nonprofits but wanted to see more long-term commitment to the reentry issue. There was also a belief that there was a need for the involvement of faith institutions and grassroots community organizations in the reentry process.

In the area of community attitudes, the stakeholders perceived a lack of awareness in the community regarding the issue of prisoner reentry. They also felt that there was a general feeling of fear and hostility toward persons who had been incarcerated. It was also suggested that the opinions of community members depend on personal experiences with the criminal justice system and with persons who have been incarcerated. Many thought that involving the community and its leaders in the reentry process could be helpful in addressing the issues of community attitudes.

While the stakeholders believed that the issues of reentry were primarily the responsibility of the criminal justice system, there was an interest in increasing the involvement of local government, nonprofit service providers, and faith- and community-based organizations in the process.

See:

Brazzell, Diana and Nancy G. La Vigne. (2009) *Prisoner Reentry In Houston: Community Perspectives.* Washington, DC: Urban Institute.

La Vigne, Nancy G., Shollenberger, Tracey L. and Debus, Sara A. (2009) *One Year out: Tracking the Experiences of Male Prisoners Returning to Houston, Texas.* Washington, DC: Urban Institute.

Shollenberger, Tracey L. (2009) *When Relatives Return: Interviews with Family Members of Returning Prisoners in Houston, Texas.* Washington, DC: Urban Institute.

Suggested web sources for the reader:

Restorative Justice – www.restorativejustice.org/intro/
American Probation and Parole Association – www.appa-net.org
Prison Policy Initiative – www.prisonpolicy.org
Sentencing Project – www.sentencingproject.org

References

Applegate, B. L., Smith, H. P., Sitren, A. H., and Springer, N. F., 2009. "From the Inside: The meaning of probation to probationers," *Criminal Justice Review* 34(1), pp. 80–95.

Cadora, E. and Swartz, C., 2000. Community Justice Atlas. Center for Alternative Sentencing and Employment Services (CASES). Unpublished report.

Clear, T. R., Rose, D. R., and Ryder, S. R., 2000. "Coercive Mobility and the Community: The Impact of Removing and Returning Offenders," paper prepared for the Urban Institute Reentry Roundtable, October, Washington DC.

La Vigne, N. G., Brooks, L. E., and Shollenberger, T. L., 2009. *Women on the Outside: Understanding the Experiences of Female Prisoners Returning to Houston, Texas.* Research Report. Washington, DC: Urban Institute.

Manhattan Institute, 1999. "'Broken Windows' Probation: The next step in crime fighting," *Civic Report* 7 (August).

Sampson, R. J., Raudenbush, S. W., and Earls, F., 1997. "Neighborhoods and Violent Crime: A multilevel study of collective efficacy," *Science* 277 (August).

Spiegler, M. D., and Guevremont, D. C., 2003. *Contemporary Behavior Therapy.* Belmont, CA: Wadsworth.

Travis J., Solomon A., and Waul, M., 2001. *From Prison to Home: The Dimensions and Consequences of Prisoner Reentry.* Washington, DC: Urban Institute.

US Department of Justice, Office of Justice Programs, 1995. "Jails and Jail Inmates 1993–94," *Bureau of Justice Statistics Bulletin* NCJ 151651. Washington, DC: US Department of Justice.

US Department of Justice, 2001. "Prison and Jail Inmates at Midyear 2000," *Bureau of Justice Statistics Bulletin* NCJ 185989. Washington, DC: US Department of Justice.

Wilson, J. Q. and Kelling, G. L., 1982. "Broken Windows," *Atlantic Monthly* 249(3), pp. 29–38.

Zehr, H., 1989. "Justice: Stumbling toward a Restorative Ideal," in P. Arthur (ed.) *Justice: The Restorative Vision*, New Perspectives on Crime and Justice, no. 7. Akron, PA: Mennonite Central Committee Office of Criminal Justice.

Further reading

Risk assessment

Zamble, Edward and Quinsey, V. L., 1997. *The Criminal Recidivism Process*. New York: Cambridge University Press. A comprehensive review of what is known about the causes of recidivism.

Public safety

Crawford, A., 1998. *Crime Prevention and Community Safety: Politics, Policies, and Practices*. Harlow, England: Longman. A critical assessment of the social and political context of community-based public safety activity.

Lab, S. P., 1997. *Crime Prevention at the Crossroads*. Cincinnati, OH: Anderson Publishing Company. A study of effective techniques for preventing crime.

Tonry, M. and Farrington, D. P. (eds), 1995. *Building a Safer Society: Strategic Approaches to Crime Prevention*. Chicago: University of Chicago Press. A collection of comprehensive studies of the effectiveness and usefulness of various approaches to crime prevention.

Offender re-entry

Maruna, S., 2001. *Making Good: How Ex-convicts Reform and Rebuild Their Lives*. Washington, DC: American Psychological Association. A study of the ways offenders change and desist from crime.

Travis, J., Solomon, A., and Waul, M., 2001. *From Prison to Home: The Dimensions and Consequences of Prisoner Reentry*. Washington, DC: Urban Institute. A review of the research and statistics on prisoner re-entry, including an assessment of impacts on family and community.

5   The future of community justice

Community justice is a new idea. Although many of the elements of community justice have a rich heritage in social thought – reparation, community, pragmatic problem solving – the idea of community justice as an expression of criminal justice is barely a decade old. We are in a time of rapid changes in criminal justice, but nobody can know in certainty where the changes will lead. What role, if any, will community play in the development of criminal justice in coming years?

To answer this question, we must shift our level of analysis from the specific to the general. The preceding chapters investigated particular applications of community justice to the three main functions of the criminal justice system: apprehension of offenders, adjudication of charges, and imposition of sanctions – police, courts, and corrections. In this analysis, we saw that community justice concepts have begun to receive broad and serious application in each of the traditional criminal justice functions. Throughout the apparatus of criminal justice, community justice ideas are increasingly common and increasingly important as foundations for new projects and innovative practices. To understand the significance of community justice as an idea, however, requires that we reach beyond these new projects to consider the core of the idea of community justice and how it transforms the current system. In this concluding chapter, we first consider the core ideas that compose the community justice model. We then address a series of questions about community justice as a new way of doing justice. We conclude with a comment on the future of community justice.

The essentials of community justice

It might fairly be argued that community justice is far from a brand-new idea. Police have always walked beats, courts have for years tried to impose sanctions that restore the victim, and corrections has worked with offenders in the community since its earliest existence. Therefore, what makes community justice such a new thing?

A great variety of activity is offered under the community justice label: from community policing to drug courts, from neighborhood probation to zero tolerance. Does it all count as community justice? For a new idea to qualify as a community justice initiative, what must it offer as a new way of doing business?

There are three essential components of community justice: place, adding value, and public safety. Throughout this book, we have described and analyzed a large number of additional ideas important to particular community justice applications: among them are partnerships, problem solving, reinvestment, and citizen involvement. These are all key ideas in community justice thinking, but there are good examples of community justice initiatives in which one or more of these is not present. It is possible (though not necessarily advisable), for instance, to build a community justice court without community involvement; one could build a community-oriented policing approach without partnerships, and so forth. But community justice cannot occur without the three components of place, adding value, and public safety. It is the fact of place that makes the approach one of "community." It is the commitment to adding value that enables the community approach to do justice. Finally, the ultimate aim of all community justice is a better experience of public safety.

Place

Community is often used as an abstraction: the fellow feeling among people who share a personal characteristic, such as ethnicity; the sense of belongingness that comes from close associations and common experiences; the mutuality of interests that binds people together in a shared destiny. These abstractions are important, for they help us understand the intuitive appeal of the term *community*. But the term *community justice*, while it calls to mind these abstract notions, also has a concrete meaning. Community justice refers to actions that take place in a designated location, a neighborhood or section where people who live see themselves as sharing life together. Community justice takes place in a specific place.

Adding value

Most of criminal justice is about a kind of "subtraction." The police investigate crimes with the intention of finding perpetrators so that they may be removed from the streets; the courts determine who should be removed and for how long; corrections confines those who have been removed and oversees others who are in risk of removal. Communities may benefit, of course, when problematic members are removed – a kind of "adding by subtracting." But community justice stands for two additional points. First, almost all of those removed eventually return, so the question of what to do about the people who live in the community, some of whom are ex-offenders, cannot be avoided by policies that only try to remove offenders. Second, and more important, dealing with offenders is not enough. Justice requires consideration of the broader and deeper quality of life in the community. From this perspective, public safety is not just a matter of strategic subtraction, but requires attention to the improvement of what is left intact. Community justice attempts to overcome the problems that produce crime, reduce the impediments to a good quality of life that communities face, and improve the capacity of communities to become safer, better places to live and do business.

Public safety

It is possible to add value to places without doing community justice. What sets the community justice ideal apart from other philosophies of community life is that community justice is involved squarely with questions of public order and public safety. But community justice does not embrace a narrow conception of public safety, as might be suggested by simple rates of crime. Community justice is interested in public safety as a broad idea: people feel free to walk the streets without fear of harassment by anyone, criminals or agents of the state. Parents have confidence that there are good options for their children's daily activity, and young people feel that they have good choices of safe and satisfying ways of passing the time. There is vibrant social (and economic) commerce, and people feel free to pursue their dreams and aspirations. From the standpoint of community justice, public safety is not represented by an electric fence, a metal detector, or a barred window; rather, public safety exists where there is open and free social commerce without personal fear. Essential to the idea of community justice is the belief that achieving such a version of public safety is a prominent public aim.

Varieties of community justice

These three essential elements of community justice leave plenty of room for many different ways of doing the work. We can visualize many varied strategies that seek to promote public safety by adding value to places. To help illustrate this, we can investigate further the core elements described above. Place is the *setting* for community justice, and this can be any neighborhood or community small enough to have an identity as distinct from other locations (especially within the same larger town or city). Public safety refers to the *goal* of community justice; adding value refers to the *means* of community justice. This enables us to investigate various differences in means (adding value) for particular community justice locations and goals (public safety). Figure 5.1 is a depiction of a conceptual model of community justice approaches based on goals and means.

Goals continuum

The goals continuum provides two extreme values. On the one hand, there is an emphasis on the goal of crime prevention; on the other, is community capacity. Community justice initiatives that emphasize the goal of crime prevention tend to identify particular types of criminal activity that trouble a community and then seek to resolve problems that make that crime tend to occur. When community justice initiatives work at this end of the continuum, they may target serious crime (such as burglaries or robberies) or broken windows offenses (such as prostitution or open drug markets) or even try to break up gangs, but their aim is always to eradicate a criminal activity. At the other end of the continuum, the concern for community capacity aims to create better community life by improving some aspect of the community's functioning. A prime example is the desire to

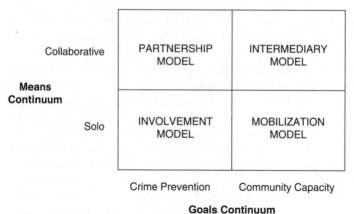

Figure 5.1 A conceptual model of community justice strategies

promote the kind of collective efficacy that seems to make some communities safer places.

Means continuum

Most governmental organizations work solo in that they attend to their own responsibilities with little direct concern about the way other organizations affect and are affected by their work. Criminal justice is no exception. Working solo has its advantages. An agency working this way can quickly implement its own policies and procedures without having to consult other organizations, and it is easy to hold staff accountable for their obligations when no other organization is around to be blamed for things not going well. These advantages explain why most organizations seek to do much of their work solo, without having to deal with the involvement of other, potentially complicating, organizations. When complicated issues such as public safety are involved, there is a recognition that one organization, working alone, can have only limited success. This has led to an increasing interest in various forms of collaborative efforts to achieve community justice, where agencies form some sort of partnership or coalition that spans organization boundaries so that organizations trying to deal with similar (or related) problems can more easily work together.

Four prototypes of community justice programs: the models of community justice

Figure 5.1, which arrays the two continua of goals and means, identifies four prototypical strategies of community justice. These can best be seen not as actual examples of existing programs, but as ideal types of community justice approaches that help us develop a critical understanding of some of the variation in community justice activity. In the following discussion, the underlying importance of each of the prototypes is described, and the pros and cons of each are presented.

Involvement Model

The initial form of community justice was to seek greater citizen involvement in the work of public safety. From its first days, the community-policing movement was a call for citizens and police to work together to deal with the problems of crime and disorder in urban settings. The idea of community policing developed from an interest in having members of the community meet with the police to develop priorities for police activity in their neighborhoods. The belief was that police would be more effective, and the community better served, if the people who needed police assistance worked together with the police.

A prototype of the Involvement Model of community justice is problem-oriented policing, developed by Herman Goldstein (Goldstein 1991). In this approach, police work together with citizen groups to identify problems affecting public safety in a particular location, gather data about that problem, design a strategy to solve the problem, and implement that strategy. At each of these stages of the problem-solving approach, there is a role for citizen involvement, ranging from consultation regarding local priorities to providing feedback about the effectiveness of the implementation of solutions.

Since the development of problem-oriented policing in the late 1980s, a body of knowledge has been created that can assist police agencies and citizens in addressing issues confronting communities. The Center for Problem-Oriented Policing has compiled case studies of problems that have been addressed by police agencies throughout the United States. These case studies have been published as reference guides for police agencies who may encounter problems that have already been addressed by other agencies. The Problem-Specific Guides for Police summarize knowledge about how police can reduce the harm caused by specific crime and disorder problems. Response Guides summarize the collective knowledge from research and practice about how, and under what conditions, certain common police responses to crime and disorder do and do not work and Problem-Solving Tool Guides explain how various analytical methods and techniques can be applied to improve an understanding of crime and disorder problems. The availability of these guides allows police and neighborhoods to work more closely together to solve problems. The guides have also been helpful in moving police agencies toward the Intermediary Model which takes a macro look at community issues and increases the number of stakeholders working on the issue at hand.

As a community justice approach, the Involvement Model has a number of advantages for police and citizens alike. For police, the model provides another source of information about local public safety problems, and it is therefore a superior way to gather information about policing priorities. It also gives the police a support system in the community for police practices. Citizens who have been consulted about the priorities for police activity are more likely to understand why the police do what they do and to support the police when inevitable problems arise. Working with a closer connection to the community, police are more likely to feel community encouragement for their work, and there is a direct sense of satisfaction for police officers who are engaged with, rather than estranged from, members of the community they serve.

Inherent within this strategy is a bilateral orientation involving the community – usually represented by some leaders and spokespersons – and the justice agency, working in tandem. The fact that the justice agency is working independently of other agencies can be a strength of this approach as well. There are no boundary concerns or turf battles, one person can speak for the interests of the justice agency, and changes in justice practices or procedures can be relatively quickly achieved.

The Involvement Model is not solely a policing strategy, although that is where it has its most apparent expression. Probation departments have established community advisory boards, and community courts often work closely with citizen leadership groups. Vermont's Reparative Justice Boards are fairly pure forms of involvement, in which the citizens themselves determine the sanctions to be implemented by the corrections system. In each of these involvement strategies, the community justice managers experience a flow of information from the community to the justice process guiding their efforts, and there is a strong sense of support from the community for the actions of community justice.

However, the Involvement Model has weaknesses. Indeed, one of its strengths – that a single agency can act unilaterally with citizen groups – is also a weakness. Often, a neighborhood suffering from deficient public safety faces complex problems, and other agencies – social services, child protection, the courts, and so forth – have responsibilities that bear on the problem at hand. Moreover, the local residents may not always speak for all the groups affected by public safety concerns in those areas. For instance, businesses, churches, and schools typically have important interests to consider in any public safety agenda facing a troubled neighborhood. For a single agency, such as the police or probation, to try to confront those problems without considering the interests of the other groups involved can reduce the impact of the community justice work and lead to frustration for the justice agency and disappointment for the citizens. The recognition that public safety problems extend to relationships beyond those between community residents and a single justice agency has led to an increasing interest in strategies involving partnerships.

Partnership Model

Under the Partnership Model, justice agencies such as the police work in collaboration with citizens and other public- and private-sector interests to identify problem priorities and generate strategic solutions to prevent crime. This approach recognizes that almost any crime or disorder problem facing a community raises the practical concerns of groups other than justice agencies and residents. If there is a problem of homelessness, for example, the local shelters will be involved, as will welfare agencies and religious groups. If there is a problem involving gangs, there is a need to consult with schools, family services, and juvenile probation. In both cases, problems of unemployment and inadequate job skills raise the possibility that businesses (as employers) and job-development services will need to be a part of the solution.

There are four layers of partnerships that justice agencies engage in. The first is the most obvious: the resident groups. Justice agencies may align their efforts with neighborhood councils, neighborhood development corporations, or citizen volunteer groups and use these partnerships to gain credibility with the community. This layer of partnership is essential to community justice: without the involvement of the community, any new initiative is not likely to represent community justice.

A second level of partnership occurs when one criminal justice agency aligns with another to try to increase the effectiveness of public safety efforts. A common example is police–probation partnerships to work with offenders under supervision in the community. A community court can also form a centerpiece for a collaborative effort between probation and police to improve the services to a neighborhood. Police–prosecution partnerships are also common.

A third level of partnership involves nonjustice governmental agencies in public safety collaborations. Probation will often work with mental-health agencies in a particular neighborhood, police will become aligned with child-protective services in a given housing project, or the domestic-violence prevention services will become a partner with police and probation in a troubled section of a city. Community schools are another common partner for police, probation, and even the courts. In these collaborations, agencies that share some responsibility for a given problem in a particular neighborhood or local setting will, instead of working independently, coordinate efforts through a cross-agency management team or a local coalition.

The final level of partnerships involves the private sector. Businesses are natural public safety partners because they have a strong interest in safe environments for commerce. Moreover, community foundations and other philanthropies can also become active in supporting innovative community justice practices that require new funding for start-up. It is also possible to have private volunteer groups, such as the chamber of commerce or the Kiwanis Club, become an active sponsor in this kind of effort.

A good example of the collaborative type of public safety effort is the Ten Points Coalition in Dorchester, Massachusetts. Led by a group of ministers, the coalition brings criminal justice representatives from all parts of the criminal justice system (police, courts, and corrections, including local, state, and federal) together with an array of social services, local citizen leaders, and private-sector representatives to work to combat gang violence. The criminal justice involvement was to target gang gun violence by focusing efforts to investigate, prosecute, and punish those gang members who used guns. Social-service agencies provided gang members with viable alternatives to gang membership and involvement, so that when pressured, they could see ways out of their gang memberships.

Citizens, led by ministers, supported the families whose children were involved in gangs and mobilized community understanding and support for the initiative. The private sector lent financial assistance to the effort (Van Beiman 1998).

The results of the Ten Points Coalition in Dorchester demonstrate the cooperative advantage that the Partnership Model has over other models: it has a much stronger capacity for overcoming the public safety problem it is designed to reduce. In Boston, partly as a result of the work of the coalition, gang homicides went from more than 10 per month to less than 10 per year. Partnerships work because they bring to bear on a complex problem an array of resources, finding multiple avenues for addressing the full range of complex issues involved in public safety.

The great advantage of the Partnership Model, that it offers a far more sophisticated response to complicated and sometimes entrenched problems, is now widely accepted. Most community justice initiatives today are not enterprises of single justice–citizen partnerships, but rather employ multiple partnerships to achieve their ends. Police rarely work alone, but typically work with one or more partners – probation, schools, businesses, religious groups – to increase the scope and flexibility of what can be done.

Partnerships have proven to be quite successful, but they are not without their own problems. Many of the agencies trying to work together are funded by the same sources, and there is a natural sense of rivalry among them for public support and funds. Moreover, years of isolation from one another may have created a history of conflict: police may distrust social services, and private businesses may distrust the justice system. Finally, there is a natural tension between organizations whose mission is to "help" and organizations set up to investigate, accuse, and punish, and this conflict in missions has to be resolved.

The main difficulty, however, relates to the limited capacity of those neighborhoods with the greatest public safety problems. Places that suffer great deficits in public safety are also usually quite poor. They lack economic infrastructure because they have few businesses and serve as home to many people who are unemployed. Drugs are far easier to obtain than jobs. Few families are intact, and adults who work generally face severe demands for their time. They spend most of their time trying to make ends meet and engaging in child care. There is little time available for voluntary participation in community projects, and there may also be very limited confidence in the ability of service agencies and justice to affect problems of the neighborhood. Morale is low.

In such places – places with insufficient *collective efficacy* – there is not much basis for collective action. People tend to mind their own business. There is often suspicion of the government and its agencies, but widespread suspicion or indifference to their neighbors, as well. People are frequently cynical about the motives of social services and justice, and they have plenty of experience to justify the cynicism. Getting participation in these locations is always hard work, and it takes time.

For these reasons, newer community justice initiatives have sought not simply to prevent crime, but to strengthen the capacity of the communities within which they work. These approaches see public safety as a long-term issue of community functioning rather than a short-term issue of community circumstances.

Mobilization Model

The earliest form of community action was community mobilization, which traces its roots to Saul Alinsky's Back of the Yards Project (Alinsky, 1991) in poor Chicago neighborhoods. Mobilization seeks to counter the most prominent problem underlying poor neighborhoods: disorganization. The essence of the mobilization approach is to bring people together to confront their own problems, to organize people with respect to the quality if their lives. The idea is that people who live in poor places cannot rely upon outsiders' altruism for an improvement of their conditions. They have to take their destiny into their own hands.

With regard to public safety, mobilization is an attractive idea. The image of residents of poor places coming together to make their neighborhood safer is an appealing one, and numerous attempts to do so have occurred. The archetypal mobilization strategy is Neighborhood Watch. Here, citizens band together to keep an eye on one another's property and children, making sure that strange people and "undesirables" are not able to put them in danger. Usually, a Neighborhood Watch campaign is kindled by the work of a single authority – the police, a neighborhood citizen's group, or another governmental agency.

The theory underlying mobilization strategies is that these approaches work by creating new capacity within neighborhoods. Neighborhood Watch, for example, builds new relationships among neighbors, even if that means no more than the occasional communication about some event that occurred in the area. Other Mobilization Model public safety programs have impact on community capacity. The neighborhood probation centers in Phoenix, Arizona, offer literacy programs for residents who are not themselves on probation. La Bodega de la Familia, a family drug-treatment center operating in the Lower East Side of Manhattan, provides drug-rehabilitation services to children and partners in families with someone under supervision of the criminal justice system.

Neighborhood-organization strategies have a spotty history. For one thing, any attempt to improve a neighborhood's capacity must build upon something, and the places that most need improvement are also places that have the least foundation to start with. It is an uphill battle to get residents of these places ready and able to come together to work on their area's problems. When the people who live or work in these places are struggling just to make it from day to day, it is unrealistic to expect them to easily make room in their lives for a whole new set of activities, especially when they do not see a likelihood for immediate payoff to their community involvement.

Often, the way to get a poor community mobilized is to inflame a sense of anger about an event or the conditions that exist, and to use the anger to get a group to "march on City Hall" and demand changes. Such confrontational strategies can generate a lot of interest and action by residents at first, but it is very hard to sustain interest or motivation after the first few public happenings. People work out their anger, and it subsides; or they see that the protest seems to bring only resistance, with little evidence of changes. They easily become discouraged. The "protest" ends, and things go back to the way they were. In other cases, the group involved in confrontational tactics may find that they become a target of lawmakers or the general public. This was evidenced by reaction to tactics utilized by the Association of Community Organizations for Reform Now (ACORN) in 2009. Federal lawmakers targeted the actions of the group and accused it of voter registration fraud. With the ensuing investigations swaying general public opinion of the group and lawmakers threatening to cut off any federal funding being received by the organization, attention moved from the work ACORN was doing to defending the image of the organization.

This is the reason why those who seek to produce public safety through improved community capacity today seek to build coalitions of efforts aimed at improvements in multiple aspects of community life. In this strategy, a central group working on behalf of the neighborhood seeks to bring various interests together to help improve community life and works to coordinate the activities of groups and resources already involved in the community. The role is one of developmental intermediary, serving to link external resources to local interests.

Intermediary Model

The Intermediary Model operates under two assumptions. First, what troubled neighborhoods need most is investment in capacity so that new strengths can be created and the natural base can be augmented. Second, ironically, what troubled neighborhoods have is a large contingent of uncoordinated, largely ineffective agencies and services involved in community life but not affecting it very much. From this point of view, what is needed most in any strategy to improve community capacity is not really *new* services, but *reinvestment* of existing resources to more directly target the needs of the community.

For the most part, intermediaries comprise local groups with resident leaders, such as a neighborhood development corporation or a local development council, that have already been active in advancing other neighborhood interests, notably housing, health care, and economic development. The intermediaries now address the problem of public safety in the same way as previous problems, by working with governmental and nonprofit groups to develop strategies for neighborhood improvement in the particular priority areas. The intermediary group then turns its attention to the work of criminal justice agencies in its community and builds collaborations with police, courts, and corrections representatives to the neighborhood, seeking ways to reorganize the efforts of those agencies to deal with particular public safety problems.

The Intermediary Model, therefore, does not spring up spontaneously, nor is it born in the planning of a particular criminal justice agency. Rather, this model represents a natural evolution of action for both the neighborhood group and the criminal justice (and other) services working in that neighborhood. (A description of how this model works is provided in the Appendix.) These approaches do not emanate from outside the neighborhood but come from a natural interest of the neighborhood in taking action on public safety priorities.

Because intermediaries are not from the criminal justice system, they tend to develop public safety strategies that are different from typical crime-prevention approaches of criminal justice. They might initiate a new recreational program to occupy the free time of local youth; develop a drop-in center and a mentoring program for youths with insufficient parental supervision; provide educational day care so single parents can work; or support a police–probation partnership that provides employment to those in re-entry and makes sure they obtain decent housing under circumstances that will reintegrate them into community life. Local intermediaries can also work closely with local resources, such as businesses and religious institutions, to find places for ex-offenders to have positive community ties. Because the intermediary is operating in a neighborhood where ex-offenders are familiar to the residents and where they probably have family, the level of anti-offender sentiment in the community can often be lower, and it is easier to generate support for reintegration programs. The work of the intermediary, then, is to help criminal justice and other governmental agencies to shift from a business-as-usual method of merely dealing with criminal events to a new way of working that seeks to strengthen the neighborhood. There is little evaluative track record for the Intermediary Model, because it is the newest approach to community justice. On the positive side, most community initiatives are moving in the direction of this approach. Rather than making unilateral efforts, criminal justice agencies are increasingly working in partnership with existing community groups and important nonprofit and public collaborators. More and more, the orientation of justice innovation is to strengthen the capacity of the community to deal with its public safety issues in addition to providing crime-prevention services. On the negative side, coordinating the agendas of the multiple agencies involved in serving a single location is a difficult task. For a local neighborhood group to be able to devote sufficient effort to the task requires more than just a handful of eager volunteers; it needs a core leadership for the long term. This implies a funding source, usually some form of governmental grant or subsidy, and once again the problem arises that the neighborhoods most in need of gaining this new capacity are also least capable of securing the kind of funding that enables the capacity to be built.

Which community justice model is best?

These four models serve as stereotypes for a wide range of community justice initiatives around the country. Which is best? There is no right answer to this question, because there is no obviously superior community justice approach. Each of these models has strengths and weaknesses. The "right" way for a community to do community justice depends upon a number of factors facing that community, including those related to the following questions.

- *How difficult is the public safety problem?* Long-term, complex problems require a larger investment from more resources working in partnership in order to achieve change. Targeted, new problems may be overcome with simpler strategies developed by a single organization.

- *How ready are the justice agencies to collaborate?* Turf battles abound in local criminal justice activity: police distrust the courts (and probation), parole is at odds with treatment providers, and so on. At its most basic, these organizations often compete with one another for funding. Unless these agencies can share a vision for community justice, effective collaboration faces long odds.
- *Is there an active, effective community leadership available to take on the problem?* In communities with strong community leaders, government agencies can rely upon those leaders to effectively involve the community. When leaders (or their organizations) are not present, it is much more difficult to develop strong, reliable partners for public safety initiatives.
- *What natural private partners exist?* Are there local businesses in the neighborhood that have an interest in promoting public safety? Is there a community foundation that can contribute to the effort?
- *What has been tried before; what are the untapped ideas?* In places where there is a history of failure, it can be difficult to generate an interest in new attempts to change the circumstances that cause problems in the community. Moreover, it is important not to try ideas that have already failed: new ideas are at a premium, and new partnerships can help to seed them.

In the end, the key strategy for community justice is the one that best fits the needs and assets of the community. This means that any successful community justice effort will begin with a careful assessment of the needs and assets a community offers, so that promising opportunities can be identified and probable dead ends avoided.

Issues in community justice

Community justice is an attractive idea but is not always accepted as a solution. Critics of community justice raise the following questions.

Is it fair to have poor places take on their own crime-prevention issues? Some people say that community justice puts too much of the public safety burden on the poorest places, where the least capacity exists to take on the problems that lead to crime. Instead of the traditional approach, they say the community justice approach turns some of the responsibility over to the people who live there, asking that they provide assistance to various agencies that engage in public safety activity.

To some people, this seems like "blaming the victim." In those areas where the public safety needs are the greatest, and where the formal criminal justice system has most failed in its community mandate, it seems somewhat unfair to expect people to promote their own safety. This is especially problematic, because as we have repeatedly noted, these are precisely the locations that have the fewest social resources and where residents are most challenged to make it from one day to the next. Placing some of the responsibility for public safety on these citizens will, some say, inevitably set the stage for the criminal justice system to point the finger at them when crime rates fail to drop. When the crime rates stay high because the community lacks the capacity to eradicate the social problems that produce crime, they suffer a cycle of crime and get the blame for it.

Community justice approaches cannot be used as an excuse for abandoning an interest in these troubled neighborhoods. The reverse must be true. The current criminal justice approach is not working, and so a greater investment is needed. What is required is a redoubling of traditional justice system efforts, not a divestment of them to community members.

Can there be equality across places? The essence of community justice is to deal with different neighborhoods in a given jurisdiction differently, depending upon the problems that each location faces. It is dangerous to start making distinctions across communities that are covered by the same laws, especially when one of the main characteristics distinguishing some communities from others is the level of concentration of minority groups and the poor. Critics of community justice wonder if "different" treatment will eventually lead to "lesser treatment" for these places.

This is a realistic concern. The places targeted for community justice initiatives have limited political and social resources. Compared to more advantaged locations, these areas have trouble getting their fiscal and programmatic priorities at the head of the line for resources. There are often few strong advocates for these locations, and other areas are typically more easily able to influence the policies that affect their lives. The nature of advantages in social capital is that some places can exert influence on their critical environment more than others. Without social capital, poor places infused with disadvantage have trouble competing for public resources.

This means that community justice initiatives could easily become common in the less troubled areas, where citizens are organized enough to demand responsiveness from the criminal justice system. Because community justice embraces the need for criminal justice to operate differently from one place to another, the fear is reasonable that for poor places, these differences will not work out to their advantage.

The criticism based on inequality raises an important, indeed a central, issue: inequality causes crime, and so public safety cannot be promoted by policies that further exacerbate the consequences of inequality. If community justice stands not just for different attention to some troubled areas, but also means more resources for those locations, then it can provide hope for a better justice system response to public safety concerns. Otherwise, areas already suffering from reduced official impact will be likely to receive not just different services, but below-standard services.

Can there be impartiality in cases? One of the most important values that underlies our contemporary criminal justice system is impartiality. This is the most democratic of our basic values because it requires that all people be treated equally without regard for their status: rich or poor, famous or ordinary. An impartial justice system is one that will have no social axe to grind, no political agenda to advance. It will merely enforce the law. The right of impartiality gives every citizen a guarantee of fairness and the expectation that no one's status will be elevated above anyone else's.

Some wonder if community justice can be impartial, considering the target at which it aims. Because the target is the quality of life in a particular location, it has to be, say some, partial to the people who live in that location. It has to place the needs and interests of the people who live and work in the community justice area as superior to those of others living or working elsewhere. In this way, community justice faces an impartiality challenge. In cases where a community justice area resident faces a conflict with a person from somewhere else, the community justice approach will, it is said, naturally tend to give higher consideration to the resident.

The loss of impartiality would be a severe price to pay for community justice, if this were true. Nobody wants a criminal justice system that gives one person an advantage over another merely because of where the person resides or who the person's neighbors are. Community justice initiatives need to find ways to advance the interests of the community without giving some people privileges. The paradox is that community justice seeks to give the residents of some communities a head start in achieving public safety, but this cannot be done at the expense of some other area. There is no obvious way to prove that community justice does not advantage some places at the expense of others, but any other situation would also raise problems of fairness.

How do you protect the rights and interests of individuals and community minorities? We all live in communities, and we all live better lives when our communities are strong, but few of us want to subjugate our personal dreams and aspirations to the community's quality of life. Community justice seeks to establish a stronger foundation of collective life so that individuals may prosper. Critics wonder if systems of government that emphasize the interests of the collective are likely to undermine the purposes of individuals to achieve the broader focuses of community life.

Trying to advance the interests of communities always raises the possibility of affecting the rights of individuals, especially when those individuals are somehow "different." Should a community be allowed to come together to stop some individuals from engaging in activities that are entirely legal but are upsetting to the dominant majority of the community? This is an issue that continuously arises in America, where personal freedom is so important. If the neighbors generally like peace and quiet, should they be able to prevent young people from getting together on a street corner? If local residents do not like activity late at night, can they prevent businesses from staying open past a certain "reasonable" hour? And if the residents can band together to enforce these types of preferences, what happens if the majority do not want some particular religious group to establish its temple, or they resent the presence of some ethnic group's social club?

Community justice is about public safety through community capacity, but it cannot be a way for a community to act out its prejudices and bigotry. Community justice can never supersede the basic protections of the Constitution and the Bill of Rights. After all, a community that does not allow *all* its residents' basic rights to be protected can never be considered "just." The ultimate aim of community justice is not merely safer places, but places where justice prevails. Safety is an essential element of justice, but achieving a safer environment at the expense of justice is no bargain.

Aren't there big problems in reinvestment strategies? Community justice seeks to reallocate public safety investments from traditional criminal justice activity toward community-focused activity. This is easier to accomplish with some justice functions than with others. For example, police already expend their resources at the community level, so for them the community justice movement is primarily a matter of shifting from traditional paramilitary policing models toward more community-oriented models, and this shift has been occurring broadly. For the courts, the shift to community can bring up additional costs, when new courtrooms are opened up to serve community and neighborhood interests. But these costs are in fact reduced because the new courts handle their fair share of cases and reduce the caseloads of other courts.

The toughest resource–redistribution problem arises in regard to corrections. The greatest correctional costs apply to prisons; by comparison, probation and parole – the obvious community options – are as little as one-twentieth the cost per case. As the preceding chapter showed, the most correctional dollars, by far, go to support incarceration. This means that the only way to reinvest this money into community settings is to move offenders, who would otherwise have been in prison, to the community. Without this, community justice correctional programs require new funding.

Moving offenders from the prison to the community happens, of course, every time an offender completes the prison sentence, and this will apply to at least 95 percent of sentenced offenders. The problem comes when trying to change the sentence either by keeping the offender in the community instead of going to prison or by getting the release to occur earlier in the sentence. There are two reasons why this is not easy to do. First, community pressures often make it harder to choose community sanctions in place of incarceration. Second, there are powerful financial interests that want to maintain a large prison population: the "prison–industrial complex" that constructs and staffs the prison. As long as prisons remain a boom industry, these interests remain strong.

In order to overcome these impediments, community justice leaders must deal with each directly. To confront community attitudes, there is a need to involve residents in the planning of the community justice correctional strategies. This will reduce the impact of fear and give residents confidence they can build community justice programs that enhance community safety rather than endanger it. Second, the resources that go to incarceration need to be thought of as being shifted to new investment opportunities with financial interests at stake in the community context. This provides incentives for an interest group coalition to push for community justice reinvestment.

Will it work, or will it backfire? The point of all these criticisms is that community justice represents a change in and a challenge to the status quo. As long as we are aware of what the status quo really is, some of these criticisms are less compelling. For example, it is easy to wonder if disadvantaged areas will suffer if the new approaches allow them to be treated differently from the more advantaged places, but the truth is that they are *already* treated differently than those areas. People who live in those places know they are treated less well than people who live elsewhere: they get less enthusiastic, less effective service from the justice system; they have more trouble meeting their individual needs; they get less consideration in political circles than do other places. Community justice can backfire, but the current system, it must be admitted, already leaves these places at a disadvantage in terms of services and safety. This cannot be changed without upsetting the status quo.

Nevertheless, there remains an all-too-common theme in justice reform that highly touted reform efforts often fall far short of their promise. This, too, could be the fate of community justice. Surface changes in criminal justice are common, but purposeful, fundamental changes in criminal justice are much harder to achieve. The criminal justice system tends to respond more readily to external forces, such as Supreme Court decisions or shifts in public opinion, than it does to the decisions of criminal justice planners and managers. To the extent that community justice remains an initiative of the criminal justice system, it risks being reconciled to this pattern of failed promises. If community justice can be a manifestation of the interests and influences of the community movement that is so prominent in other arenas, fundamental change in criminal justice may occur.

How will community justice initiatives be measured to ensure funding is received? In order to make decisions about funding for programs and staff, government and nonprofit sources will look to the effectiveness of proposed and existing programs to justify providing funding. Criminal justice organizations have traditionally utilized numerically based evaluation systems to measure achievement. Using an evaluation system that is solely based upon numbers cannot provide a true picture of the success of community justice. Methods of evaluation will need to be arrived at through collaboration between criminal justice elements, academics, governmental agencies, and nonprofit groups. This collaboration will be important because what one element utilizes may not be acceptable to others involved in the collaborative effort. Goals and objectives must be set and it is vital to know if those goals and objectives are being met by the partners involved. As previously discussed, in most evaluation practice evaluators examine outputs, outcomes, impacts, and processes. Outputs are the goods or services that are produced by the program or project. They are usually easily measured but do not address the effect of the program or project. Outcomes are the effects of the interventions and can be measured. Measurements can provide the evaluator with information about what events or actions occurred as a result of the implementation of the program or project. Impacts are effects that are longer term and addresses broader issues beyond the specific program or project. Because impact evaluation depends more on longitudinal methods, they do not tend to provide the immediate feedback that outcome and impact evaluation can provide. Processes are the methods or mechanics used to implement and carry out the program or project. Evaluation of processes focuses on the efficiency issues relating to the program or project. In order to obtain a comprehensive evaluation of a program or project, all four evaluation methods should be utilized.

Since the United States is encountering the worst financial crisis since the Great Depression of 1929, it will be important to have agreed upon standards of measurement that can allow community justice initiatives to draw funding from all levels of government as well as the nonprofit sector. There will be much competition for scarce funds and unless the funding sources see value in programs requesting funding they will put their money elsewhere. After diverting money from policing programs funded through the Office of Community Oriented Policing (COPS Office) to Homeland Security projects due to the events of September 11, 2001, the federal government appears to be increasing funds to the COPS Office. While competition for these funds will be keen, creative projects that involve collaboration with multiple stakeholders will be positioned to have an increased chance at being awarded the necessary funding. The same process should play out in competition for funding from private grants and nonprofit sources.

The future of community justice

There is no question that community justice is no longer an emerging idea but a prominent new conceptualization of the way criminal justice ought to be delivered. Community justice has developed deep roots in police practice, informs most of the current innovation in courts, and has become an important new force in correctional practice. Almost all of the new ideas in criminal justice contain some aspect of community justice thinking: place, problem solving, partnerships, restoration, and so forth. Overall, the underlying value of community justice has developed salience in criminal justice thinking.

Yet the appeal of traditional criminal justice remains very strong. Television offers another cop chase-and-capture show every night, punitive sentencing strategies are very popular in the public mind, and the idea is widely held that public safety comes from no-holds-barred criminal justice. Criminal justice insiders know that traditional methods have significant limitations, and their growing interest in community justice stems from a sense that the practices of community justice can overcome some of those limitations. There is also a prevailing desire to work in more close cooperation with the community, rather than in isolation. These beliefs within the system have made the formerly cautious and even defensive criminal justice establishment increasingly interested in the possibilities that arise when community justice approaches are employed.

Community leaders have also started to recognize the potential of the underlying principles of community justice. Leaders seek locally relevant justice practices in which citizens have a role and for which the quality of community life is an aim. As new initiatives develop offering this as a way of providing justice services, many community leaders see the advantages and seek even wider application of these principles. With each success in community justice, resident resistance to innovation fades, and mutual support for more of these new ideas grows. The community justice movement has been strong partly because it meets the various needs of a changing justice system and an insistent public.

Community justice has been a popular idea despite the fact that evaluative evidence in support of it is scant, at best. As the previous chapters have shown, community justice makes sense from the standpoint of what we know about public safety and strong communities. There are a few significant evaluation studies that confirm the wisdom of some of the community justice conceptual foundations: community policing has paid dividends in law enforcement; community courts and special courts (such as drug courts) have developed impressive track records; restorative justice offers sufficient benefits to encourage expansion of the idea. The empirical foundation for a community justice movement, however, is not as strong as any of these parts.

A core aspect of the future of community justice, then, is evidence. New initiatives must be studied and their results more fully understood. The relative benefits of different strategies of community justice need to be documented so that an informed conception of community justice priorities can be developed. This will not happen rapidly but will require sustained attention to the benefits and costs of community justice activity.

A second aspect of the future of community justice is political. A great deal will depend upon whether the current coalescence of opinion in favor of community justice concepts will continue. Today, there is a broad consensus of opinion among criminal justice leaders, researchers, and community leaders that the potential of community justice justifies continued interest and experimentation. New programs have solid support among the key constituencies needed to sustain community justice action. But the criminal justice system has a way of shifting its attention from time to time, and when the inevitable shift occurs, the momentum of community justice will be tested. If the basic support for community justice continues, this shift in interest will not be a problem; if the support evaporates when the attention shifts, community justice will struggle to survive.

Finally, there is the question of whether this new idea called community justice can retain its quality of creativity and innovation. Central to the idea of community justice is a challenge to the inventive capacities of collaborative partnerships of citizens and justice officials working together on the problems that face a particular geographic area. The idea is to avoid the routine response to crime and instead to invent new ways of responding to the challenge of public safety. It is easy to develop a copycat version of community justice, where local partnerships try to re-create the experiences of other areas rather than produce their own. Community justice will endure so long as the innovative and inventive spirit that fueled its inception supports its continuation.

In some ways, this book has been entirely about the future of community justice. Every idea presented in this book is a conception about how the future of criminal justice could be changed by a commitment to the values and vision of community justice.

References

Alinsky, S. [1946] (1991) *Reveille for Radicals*, reissue, New York: Random House.
Goldstein, H. (1991) *Problem Oriented Policing,* New York: McGraw Hill.
Van Bieman, D. (1998) "In Search of Moses," *Time Magazine* 152 (December 14).

Further reading

Bazemore, G. (1995) "Rethinking the Sanctioning Function in Juvenile Court: Retributive or Restorative Responses to Youth Crime," *Crime and Delinquency* 41, pp. 296–316.

Clear, Todd R. and Karp, D. R. (1999) *The Community Justice Ideal: Preventing Crime and Achieving Justice*. New York: Westview Press.

Clear, Todd R. and Rose, D. (1999) "When Neighbors Go to Jail: Impact on Attitudes about Formal and Informal Social Control," *Perspectives in Justice*. Washington, DC: US Department of Justice, Office of Justice Programs, National Institute of Justice.

Decker, Scott H. and Van Winkle, B. (1996) *Life in the Gang: Family, Friends and Violence*. New York: Cambridge University Press.

Karp, David R., ed. (1998) *Community Justice: An Emerging Field*. Lanham, MD: Rowman and Littlefield.

Rose, Dina R. and Clear, T. R. (1998) "Incarceration, Social Capital and Crime: Examining the Unintended Consequences of Incarceration," *Criminology* 36(3), pp. 441–79.

Sampson, R. J., Morenoff, J. D., and Earls, F. (1999) "Beyond Social Capital: Spatial Dynamics of Collective Efficacy for Children," *American Sociological Review* 64, pp. 633–60.

Smith, M. and Clear, T. R. (1997) Fathers in Prison: Interim Report. Draft report to the Edna McConnell Clark Foundation by the Rutgers University School of Criminal Justice.

Smith, M. E. and Dickey, W. J. (1998) "What If Corrections Were Serious about Public Safety?," *Corrections Management Quarterly* 2(3), pp. 12–30.

Mobilization

Merry, S. E. and Milner, N. (1993) *The Possibility of Popular Justice: A Case Study of Community Mediation in the United States*. Ann Arbor: University of Michigan Press. Investigates the circumstances leading to and consequences of a community-based alternative to the formal legal system for solving local conflicts.

Podolefsy, A. (1983) *Case Studies in Community Crime Prevention*. Springfield, IL: Charles C. Thomas. Demonstrates a series of ways that communities can systematically come together to prevent crime.

Partnerships

Crawford, A. (1997) *The Local Governance of Crime: Appeals to Community and Partnerships*. Oxford, England: Clarendon. Describes the conceptual and practical limits of community-based crime-prevention partnerships.

Politics of crime prevention

Chambliss, W. J. (2001) *Power, Politics, and Crime*. Boulder, CO: Westview. A critical analysis of the way political interests affect the formulation of crime policy.

Miller, L. L. (2001) *The Politics of Community Crime Prevention*. Burlington, VT: Ashgate Dartmouth. Description of the politics of the Federal Government's Weed and Seed program, in which law enforcement (Weed) is coupled with community services (Seed).

Appendix

Community justice as a strategy: how CASES makes it work

A team of correctional professionals at CASES (Center for Alternative Sentencing and Employment Services) has recently undertaken a community justice project that begins by responding to the kinds of questions that are raised by community justice. Unlike other strategies, such as community court or community policing, the CASES approach is not linked to a particular criminal justice agency. Rather, it begins with "the problem" and "the place" and develops a comprehensive community justice strategy tailored to each community it serves.

The CASES philosophy is as follows:

The PURPOSE of community justice is to improve the long-term public safety of areas hard hit by crime through developmental approaches that increase the community capacity and well-being of people who live and work in those places.

The METHOD of community justice is to reinvest public resources in public safety strategies that build stronger community life.

The PRINCIPLES of community justice are as follows:

- Share decision making between criminal justice professionals and community leaders.
- Coordinate cross-agency criminal justice responses to community priorities.
- Merge criminal justice investments and community resources locally.
- View offenders as untapped resources.

To implement this philosophy, the CASES team includes, in addition to a project manager, a community organizer, a program developer, and a data mapper. Using the skills represented by this set of specializations, the CASES team addresses community justice from a unique perspective. Using the skills represented by this set of specializations, the CASES team addresses community justice from a unique perspective. CASES designs community justice to work through the partnerships between the criminal justice system and the residents and businesses in the community. These partnerships have two effects. First, they provide a vehicle for residents to make their neighborhood's priorities a part of the justice response at their location. Second, the participation of residents in the processes of justice enables the justice system to achieve a new level of credibility with the residents in the area it serves. The experience of just about every community justice initiative is this two-pronged result: a shift in the priorities of justice and a growth in the credibility of justice.

The new priorities typically involve a variety of programmatic emphases. A partial list of the kinds of new ideas promoted by citizen partnerships would include the following:

- An emphasis on *prevention* that provides programs and supports for at-risk youth and their families.
- Changes in the *physical aspects* of the neighborhood – graffiti, debris, dilapidates housing, abandoned lots, etc. – that so often contribute to a sense of diminished safety.
- Victim restoration strategies that enable the offender to make direct *reparation* to the victim and the community.
- Support systems for *returning offenders* whose successful adjustment to the community will do so much to improve community life.

Community justice initiatives are not arrest focused. They are oriented toward *problem solving:* they try to identify the conditions that contribute to diminished public safety and determine how they can be overcome. Because citizens are involved in that process, a much richer, more comprehensive, and more promising set of answers can be developed.

In the end, community justice is a set of programs that operates at the community level. But these programs are not simply the brainchild of the criminal justice agencies involved, nor are they reproductions of strategies undertaken elsewhere. They are place specific, designed to confront problems particular to the location for which they are designed. They use citizens as resources in implementation – they leverage resources by partnering with residents, businesses, and other governmental services so that a broader, more complete program is developed. Finally, the measure of success of these programs is not "more criminal justice" as is often the case in traditional programming, but "less need for criminal justice," as public safety problems begin to be resolved.

Community justice initiatives in the CASES model work through three independent strategies: partnership development, information analysis and mapping, and resource leveraging.

Partnership development

There is usually a degree of mistrust and misunderstanding between the criminal justice system and the residents of the communities in which justice actions are concentrated. Community justice initiatives cannot be effectively undertaken until this distrust and misunderstanding are addressed.

CASES begins its work with an assessment phase that involves up to six months or more of intensive interviewing in the community and among justice officials. During this process, CASES officials get to know the key people in the community and in the justice system and learn about their point of view on the need for new approaches to justice in that area. This lengthy process may seem to delay the project, but it is actually an essential way to develop the foundation for effective partnerships. CASES seeks to understand the differences and common-alities in points of view, the potential areas of consensus, and the likely active individuals in the innovations that will be undertaken.

Among the people involved in this assessment process will be the resident leaders, whose opinions are seen as important in the neighborhood, financial part-ners, who might be willing to support some aspects of the new programs, and justice innovators, who will be willing to take an imaginative view of their invest-ments in the neighborhood. From these three elements will be built an effective partnership strategy that can bring a comprehensive community justice strategy to the neighborhood.

It is only after this initial phase of assessment is completed that the first meet-ings of community members and justice official take place. In this way, the CASES strategy differs from many community justice approaches that *begin* with a big meeting of the stakeholders. If such a meeting occurs too soon in the process, it can lead to unresolvable conflicts or a sense of frustration that impedes the aims of collaboration. The CASES approach, referred to as "consensus organ-izing," sees the meeting and planning phases of the community justice project as intermediate stages in the change process, only to be undertaken after the CASES team has established good, one-on-one working relationships with all major stakeholders.

Information analysis

The community justice orientation to a particular place requires a major shift in thinking for everyone concerned. Criminal justice officials and residents alike are used to thinking about criminal cases – offenders and crimes – but they find it hard to replace that emphasis with one on "location." The best way to help people develop a "place" frame of reference is through the use of maps.

A good map, like many a picture, is better than a thousand words. Maps that show offenders in concentration in a neighborhood demonstrate startlingly why merely arresting more residents cannot, by itself, add much to community safety. A density map of crime can show why a given area deserves more attention in criminal justice investments.

But the most important maps are "resource" maps. CASES does two types of maps. The first is a map of neighborhood resources, which shows churches, schools, and other services available in the community. More interesting, some-times, are the maps of criminal justice resources devoted to the area. These maps show, block by block, how much money is currently being spent by criminal justice agencies across the neighborhood. It is the impressive number of dollars spent on current policy that sets the stage for people to think somewhere along the lines, "Surely we can get more impact for these expenditures."

The final type of information is programmatic. After leading the community justice partners through a process of analyzing information about crime and justice, a series of ideas emerges about new ways to deal with criminogenic problems in the neighborhood. These are folded into an understanding of "what works," based on various reviews of existing literature on crime prevention. The aim is to develop programs that have a proven track record, not programs that fail.

Resource leveraging

The final strategy is to find ways of expanding resources for new programs. Four sources are tapped: reinvested justice resources, resident contributions, offender contributions, and private partners.

The most significant resources are those already invested in the area by the criminal justice system. In our examples earlier, it is clear that this can amount to millions of dollars, mostly in terms of staffing. Because the bulk of these dollars is assigned to personnel, what this amounts to is reassigning works tasks of existing staff. For example, a probation agency may shift a probation officer or two from a caseload of an after-school project; a sheriff might shift a correctional officer from the cell range to an offender work project in the neighborhood.

Criminal justice agencies are, for obvious reasons, cautious about assigning staff to new tasks – each staff member was already assigned to a mandated service, and most agencies feel hard-pressed to meet existing commitments, much less take on new ones. This is where resident and offender resources contribution can play a role. Resident volunteers can take responsibilities that make it possible to free staff for new assignments, and offender labor can help pay for the costs of those reassignments. One can imagine, for example, a youth center that is staffed by criminal justice professionals but has a heavy commitment of citizen volunteers who help round out the supervision. Several of the youth who might attend such a center are those who are already on probation, thus making their "reports" to the probation officer with the caseload less important. And offenders might perform some of the routine maintenance tasks to keep the center clean and open.

Even though it is possible to leverage these existing resources, it is necessary to have unencumbered dollars available for program start-up and to support the development and organizing activities in the neighborhood. Thus, the final source of resources is a private partner who contributes financially to the innovative programming – typically a nonprofit organization or otherwise philanthropic venture. Identifying a financial partner is a key aspect of the CASES approach to community partnerships.

How does community justice look in the long term?

CASES helps the community set up an intermediary function to support community justice – a localized community justice center. The center has three capacities: citizen organizing, program development, and information analysis. The continuing function of the center is to "grow" community justice initiatives. They typically begin with a single-interest program, such as an after school project, one that will generate strong citizen support and good results for criminal justice, and can be easily put in place. From these success experiences, the center branches out to other problems, based on an assessment of the information about the community and effective working relationships with the community and criminal justice partner.

Thus, what CASES is trying to build is a long-term capacity for community justice in the form of a community justice center that operates in the neighborhood and has the capacity to generate ideas about reinvesting justice resources in new ways that promote community safety, working with citizens and justice officials to build confidence in those programs, and helping residents become more in control of the safety of the places where they live.

Index